D0614136

Battleground Europe

YPRES

Sanctuary Wood and Hooge

British aircraft behind the German lines with aircrew buried by the wreck.

SANCTUARY WOOD. HOOGE

By the same author:

Battleground Europe

*Other guides in the
Battleground Europe Series
in preparation:*

Vimy Ridge

The Somme: Beaumont Hamel

The Somme: Thiepval

The last two decades have seen an enormous increase in the numbers of visitors to the battlefields and other sites of the Western Front, that area of France and Flanders which bore the brunt of fighting during the First World War. Sadly, until now the guide books available to visitors — whether the casual tourist, the serious historian, or someone seeking the grave of or memorial to a relation — have generally been of poor quality and poorer content, often merely adding to a reader's confusion. The **'Battleground Europe'** series of guides adopts a fresh approach, providing up-to-date information about sites, routes and other details, and taking the reader on a tour of the area covered by the book. Amply supplied with illustrations and maps, each volume contains a general history as well as covering a number of actions within the area, enabling today's observer to transform the impression from one of a rural scene to one of the horrors and heroism that characterised events during the Great War. The text directs readers to certain areas and operations, allowing them to visualise what they would have seen more than seventy years ago, and incorporates those pieces of evidence, whether trench or other surviving relic, cemetery, memorial or museum, that remain today as reminders of what happened so many years ago. Each author has been selected not only for his knowledge of the area and what happened there between 1914 and 1918, but also for his knowledge of the area as it is now, making these guides indispensable for tourist and serious scholar alike.

Battleground Europe
YPRES
Sanctuary Wood and Hooge

Nigel Cave

LEO COOPER
London

First published in 1993
Reprinted and updated 1995
LEO COOPER

190 Shaftesbury Avenue, London WC2H 8JL
an imprint of
Pen & Sword Books Ltd
47 Church Street, Barnsley, South Yorkshire S70 2AS

Copyright © Nigel Cave 1993, 1995

ISBN 0 85052 355 9

A CIP catalogue record of this book is available
from the British Library

Printed by
Redwood Books,
Trowbridge, Wilts

To the memory of
Rose E. Coombs, MBE
author of *Before Endeavours Fade*
in gratitude

The name of the wood will perhaps pass down
to history; in any case, those who have been
there will remember it, and tell of it, and tell of
it while life lasts, for the shadow of its trees is
like the shadow in the valley of death

Captain Ernest White RAMC
attached 6 Durham Light Infantry
February 1916

LIST OF MAPS

BRUCE BAIRNSFATHER

DIRECTING THE WAY TO THE FRONT
"Yer knows the dead 'orse 'cross the road? Well,
keep straight on till yer comes to a prambulator
'longside a Johnson 'ole!"

These maps have come from a wide range of sources. These sources include the Official History, sketch maps from War Diaries and Regimental Histories, trench maps and others. It is rare for any two maps to agree with any great cartographical exactness, but I hope that the sketch maps will give visitors a reasonably accurate impression of what went on where. Given the tremendous changes that have taken place in this part of Belgium, it is fortunate that the ground over which this guide takes us allows us to see so much of the area, lie of the land and features, as it faced the opposing sides in the Great War.

CONTENTS

Hill 62 shortly after the war

ACKNOWLEDGEMENTS

The preparation of this book has required the assistance of a wide variety of people. In Belgium I am grateful for the help of Albert, Beke of the Cloth Hall Great War Museum and of Jacques of the Hill 62, Sanctuary Wood Museum.

From institutions I have received help from Major Tom Craze of the Royal Green Jacket Museum; and considerable assistance from Mr Steve Shannon of the Durham Light Infantry Museum; much of the credit for the chapter on the attack of 9 August, 1915, featuring the Second Battalion of that justly renowned regiment, lies with him. I am grateful to the DLI Museum for the illustrations that they have provided, above all of the cover painting of the action at Hooge, which used to hang in the 2nd Battalion Officers' Mess until its disbandment.

I am grateful to the Committee of the Western Front Association for permission to use their aerial photographs of the area covered in this book; these photographs were taken by Mr John Giles, the founder of the Association, and himself the author of most informative books on the subject of the Western Front.

I owe a special debt of gratitude to Mr Tony Spagnoly. He it was who transformed my approach to the battlefields (though I had followed my Grandfather's progress during the war over the ground with the use of his diary), and who inspired me to produce this type of guide. A tour of the battlefields with him is always an education and a moving experience.

I am grateful to a number of colleagues at Ratcliffe. Brother E. Murphy IC helped me around the mysteries of my computer; and Mr George Friendship read the initial draft and pointed out some of the more ludicrous errors and inflections of language. My pupils on a recent tour of the battlefields endured some rather eccentric stops, but seemed willing enough to pose for photographs against some significant landmark.

My father, once more, proved himself eagle-eyed in spotting errors of fact and grammar, as well as lending me precious books from his Great War library.

No book of this kind would stand much chance of sales without the work of the Commonwealth War Graves Commission and the exemplary task that is done in preserving the memory of the war dead of the Empire and Dominions. As for most authors in my position, I am indebted to the Commission and its officers, in particular Mr Jeremy Gee and Miss Beverly Webb for their time and assistance, and to the searchers in the Records Room. I am sure that I express the views of almost everyone when I say that this certainly is a department of Government that achieves its objectives, and whose efforts must leave even the most hardened moved.

I am grateful to the following publishers for permission to quote from their books: William Kimber, *Armageddon Road, A VC's Diary 1914 — 1916, Billy Congreve,* edited by Terry Norman; Sono Nis Press, *Victoria B.C., Canada The Journal of Private Fraser* edited by R. H. Roy; Cassel, *Into Battle, A Soldier's Diary of the Great War* by John Glubb.

I would like to thank Roni Wilkinson and Toby Buchan and the rest of the team at Pen & Sword in Barnsley for their help and encouragement.

This book is dedicated to Miss Rose Coombs, MBE who died in January 1991. She has opened up the Western Front to so many in her book which ensures that even the most obscure British Memorial rates a mention. She has done a great service in enabling new generations to discover the sites where their forebears fought and are commemorated.

Once more my thanks are due to Mr Mike Willis, late of the Photographic Department of the Imperial War Museum, and thanks are due to that museum for permission to reproduce certain photographs.

INTRODUCTION

In 1968 I made my first visit to the Battlefields, and Hill 62 was the first museum that I visited. Ypres and area was then a much more placid place than it is now, and it was possible to find relics of the war, such as fragments of rum jars and webbing, shrapnel and caltraps, relatively easily.

What it was not possible to do easily was to find out what exactly had happened in the area of the museum at Hill 62. In this book the ground covered is limited to just the north of the hamlet of Hooge, the eastern and southern edges of Sanctuary Wood, and to the south the large village of Zillebeke. Even in this relatively small area there was so much of incident that none of the actions of 1917 are covered, and very little of 1914.

It was from the spring to the autumn of 1915 that the name of Hooge was rarely out of the newspapers; and for a time it was probably the most feared place on the Western Front to the British soldier. The new horrors of gas and flamethrower came soon after each other in this sector, and this was added to the frightening threat of mine warfare.

The Canadians are commemorated by their memorial on Hill 62, and aspects of their action in June 1916 are covered. General Sir John Glubb first came into the Front Line here in the winter of 1915, as a young subaltern in the Royal Engineers. He describes his time at Zillebeke and in the line in his own words. A short piece illustrates how the nature of the war changed, especially in the war of movement that characterised the summer days of 1918.

To follow what is described here can take a matter of a few hours or a day. It is hoped that the book will provide a time of interest of the person who follows it on the ground, and of education to the reader at home. Above all, I hope that it will continue to keep in the mind of today's generation the memory of men who endured the misery and destruction of the greatest conflict that had scourged mankind before the traumas of 1939.

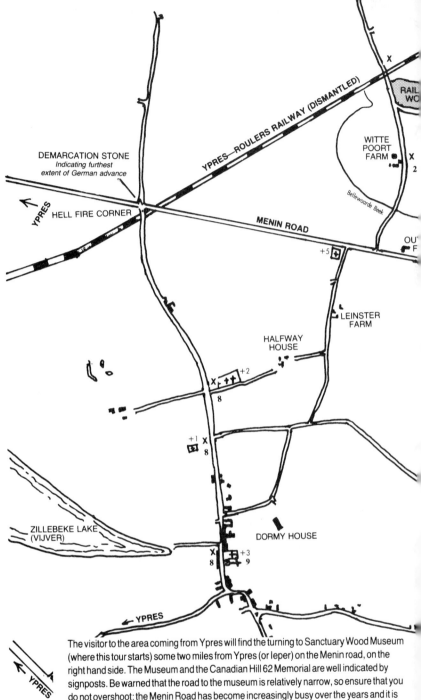

The visitor to the area coming from Ypres will find the turning to Sanctuary Wood Museum (where this tour starts) some two miles from Ypres (or Ieper) on the Menin road, on the right hand side. The Museum and the Canadian Hill 62 Memorial are well indicated by signposts. Be warned that the road to the museum is relatively narrow, so ensure that you do not overshoot: the Menin Road has become increasingly busy over the years and it is difficult to turn around again. The order of the itinerary relates directly to the chapter numbers, so that the reader should follow the numbers on the 'now' map, and read more detailed instructions at the beginning of each chapter. Potential car parking points are indicated. The hotel at Hooge has now reopened (1994) and offers the best point to park for chapters 3, 4, 5 and 6. Please ensure that permission is obtained from the proprietor if possible. At all times be aware of the cycle lanes — it is illegal to park on these in Belgium.

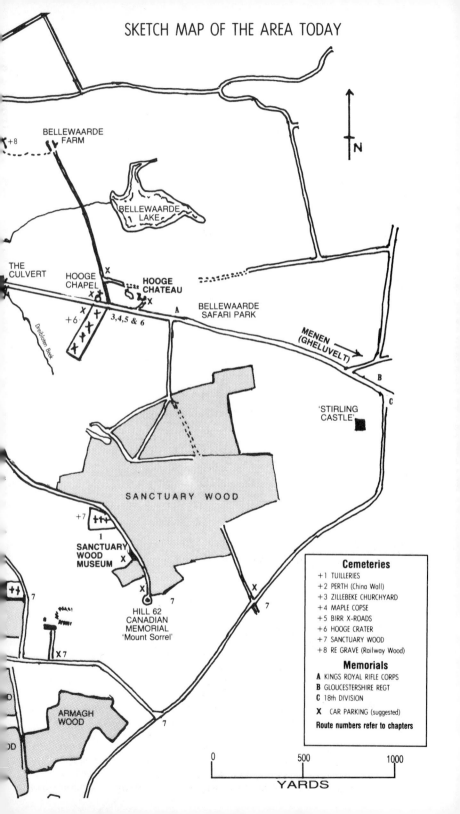

SKETCH MAP OF THE AREA TODAY

N

+8

BELLEWAARDE
FARM

BELLEWAARDE
LAKE

THE
CULVERT

HOOGE
CHAPEL

HOOGE
CHATEAU

Dreibloten Beek

+6

3,4,5 & 6

A

BELLEWAARDE
SAFARI PARK

MENEN
(GHELUVELT)

B

C

'STIRLING
CASTLE'

SANCTUARY WOOD

+7

1

SANCTUARY
WOOD
MUSEUM

X

7

7

HILL 62
CANADIAN
MEMORIAL
'Mount Sorrel'

X 7

7

ARMAGH
WOOD

7

Cemeteries
+1 TUILLERIES
+2 PERTH (China Wall)
+3 ZILLEBEKE CHURCHYARD
+4 MAPLE COPSE
+5 BIRR X-ROADS
+6 HOOGE CRATER
+7 SANCTUARY WOOD
+8 RE GRAVE (Railway Wood)

Memorials
A KINGS ROYAL RIFLE CORPS
B GLOUCESTERSHIRE REGT
C 18th DIVISION

X CAR PARKING (suggested)

Route numbers refer to chapters

0   500   1000
YARDS

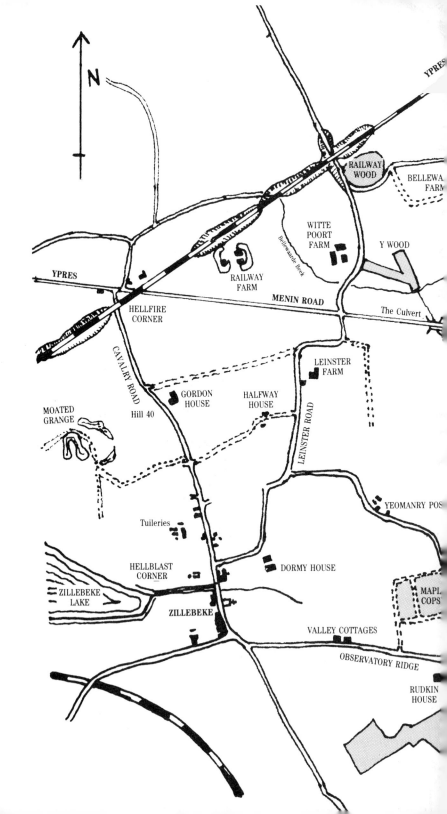

SKETCH MAP OF THE AREA DURING THE WAR

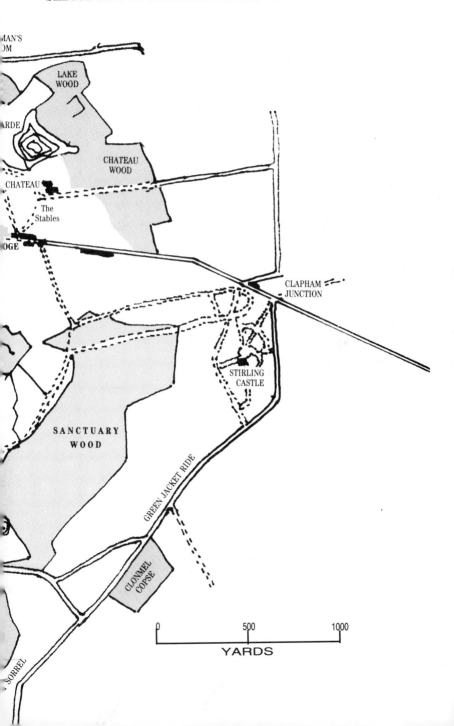

LAKE WOOD

CHATEAU WOOD

CHATEAU

The Stables

CLAPHAM JUNCTION

STIRLING CASTLE

SANCTUARY WOOD

GREEN JACKET RIDE

CLONMEL COPSE

0   500   1000

YARDS

The area around Bellewaarde Lake and the village of Hooge in 1917. Chateau Wood has been reduced to shattered stumps by artillery shells.

Men in Chateau Wood, 1917. The state of the ground gives some indication of the conditions suffered by the combatants in this part of the battlefield.

W. F. A.

A modern view of Sanctuary Wood Cemetery and the north western edge of the Wood. The museum buildings can be seen at the bottom right. It was in this area that Princess Patricia's Canadian Light Infantry fought so hard in June 1916.

SANCTUARY WOOD TODAY

The usual approach to the museum at Sanctuary Wood and Hill 62 is along the Menin Road from Ypres (or Ieper, in Flemish). There is a narrow right hand turning, Canada Lane (also known as Maple Avenue), off the Menin Road, which turning is signposted, both to the museum and, more prominently, to the Canadian Memorial on Hill 62. This road is a cul-de-sac, and is the only way in which the museum may be reached.

The newcomer to the area will, doubtless, be concentrating on his or her driving, but as a consequence will miss much of historical importance. At this stage, what should be particularly noticed is the great bulk of the wood on the left hand side of the road which comes into view after several hundred yards. The museum at Sanctuary Wood is on the south west edge of the wood, and it is not until a visitor has (subsequently) driven up to Clapham Junction and along Greenjacket Ride that a full appreciation of the size of the wood may be made. The present wood has regrown within the boundaries of the one that was blown to smithereens during the course of the Great War; thus what you see now is similar, at least in geographical area, to that seen by the British and Germans in October and November 1914.

Sanctuary Wood played no great part in the fighting of 1914; some troops were rested there, others were positioned nearby as a reserve (for example the 6th Cavalry Brigade at the end of October), and it gained its name. There is no gospel reason as to how its name came about, but soldiers were sent there if they

15

Scenes from our Daily Life.

A heart-felt cartoon by a front line soldier showing his view of Sanctuary Wood. Reproduced from the *Whizz-Bang* the monthly journal of the Durham Light Infantry, published in Belgium, 1916.

were lost and their units untraceable, whilst reserves (such as the cavalry brigade in late October) might be rested in relative safety, but with easy access to the Menin Road or south to Hill 60. As the First Battle of Ypres progressed, units became disorganised and much diminished due to casualties. A number of forces were put together to make respectably sized bodies of men that could be coherently commanded, and one of these, Bulfin's Force, (commanded by Major-General E S Bulfin) used the Wood extensively as a holding and a rest area for his troops.

The Sanctuary Wood Museum is on your right hand side, just beyond the British Cemetery. It is an excellent spot from which to commence any battlefield tour, as it combines artefacts, photographs (some of a most lurid and stomach-turning variety—but who said that war is nice?), and trenches—a taste, at least, of the Great War.

A word here about trench museums. It was inevitable—and desirable—that after the war relatives of the fallen and former soldiers would wish to see something of the battlefields where loved ones or comrades were killed. It was equally inevitable that people would also see the possibilities of making money by opening museums and cafes and charge an entrance fee. Of the number that sprang up in the immediate post-war years, this is the only one that has survived. It is still run by the same family, and is based on trenches that were part of the Vince Street and Jam Row complex of trenches dug in later 1916. Other such museums have now disappeared—in the 1930s, for example, the area around Hill 60 had trench museums that included dug outs complete with beds and equipment. These do not appear to have survived the Second World War. As a museum, the outstanding one in the area, without a doubt, is that in the Cloth Hall at Ypres, which has grown from very modest beginnings (in one of the chambers in the tower) to the fine display on view now. The major drawback, from the point of view of the British visitor, is the lack of labelling in English, although a brief hand list summary is available.

The Sanctuary Wood museum is entered via a cafe, where it is possible to purchase refreshment of the liquid kind. The proprietor is quite happy for visitors to eat their own food, and this is particularly useful if the weather happens to be unkind. (The same arrangement applies at the Queen Victoria's Rifles cafe at Hill 60). On payment of the entrance fee, the visitor goes through two exhibition rooms before going out to the trenches. The first of these rooms houses some remarkable exhibits, chief among which are the stereoscopic photographs and the headgear of various regiments.The stereoscopic photographs provide an uncanny sense of reality, bringing people and objects into three

A French howitzer guards the entrance to museum and cafe at Hill 62.

dimensions (though please note that a small proportion of people do not have stereoscopic vision). These photographs do not disguise any of the horrific aspects of the Great War, and act as something of an antedote to the present peaceful and largely pastoral nature of the battlefields. The helmets on display were worn by the various combatants, at least until steel helmets became common in 1915 and 1916. Notice that the German pickelhaube helmets were covered when in action by canvas, making the possessor rather less of a target. These helmets were highly prized as souvenirs during the war, and my grandfather was a proud owner of one. The cavalry helmets tended to be even more magnificent, but even these gave way in the course of time to the more mundane tin hat. Standard wear for the British soldier was a peaked cloth cap; the older hands soon removed the wire stiffeners from inside the brim, and shaped it to their own unique style. The German soldier wore a round cloth cap or the pickelhaube.

Other items are of interest, but it is not easy to know quite what they are apart from the obvious general description of rifle, grenade, sword or bayonet. This is another museum that suffers from the lack of labels.

The next room has displays of weapons that encompasses both World Wars. There are remnants of aircraft engines, large mortars, some uniforms, heavy and light machine guns. These are all of interest, and if nothing else provokes heated discussions as to what exactly an object is or was used for!

Before venturing outside, it would be useful to ensure that you are suitably equipped: sturdy shoes (preferably boots or wellingtons) and a torch are advised. This trench area was to the rear of the Front Line until the events of June 1916, when the Canadians were ejected by a German attack, and then subsequently recaptured the ground a few days later. This action is described in fuller detail elsewhere; certainly the ground here would have seen a lot of fighting in June 1916. The trenches that are now on view date more or less from that time, as do the two tunnels. These tunnels were in effect covered trenches, and provided rather more effective cover, though only against relatively light shelling. What it did do was hide movement in the trenches from enemy view.

One must not be misled by the remnants of the trenches that are on view now; this is only a very small part of a most complex arrangement. Even here it is clear that there were several lines to a trench system. The Front Line itself usually had saps; that is a short trench, usually quite narrow, driven out at approximately right angles from the line towards the enemy, with a single bay at the end, that provided a guard for the main system and a listening post so that the actions of the enemy in No Man's Land might be observed. The main trenches were split up into traverses —a zigzag arrangement that was designed to prevent the occupants from enfilade fire—ie fire from the side—should the enemy break into a trench and more usually from the effects of shell or mortar blast. These traverses in the Front Line were also known as Fire Trenches. The front of the trench was a parapet (in the case of the museum the side nearer the road) and the rear a parados. Shelters dug into the wall of the trench, or reached by stairs, were dug-outs. They were usually sited on the trench wall facing the enemy, preventing shells, mortars and so forth being pitched down into them. The main exception to this state of affairs came, inevitably, when one side or the other captured a trench. However any shelter, whatever the risks, was generally more than welcome in such circumstances.

On the side of the trench facing the enemy was a raised ledge, the firestep. This brought the soldier to a level where he could see enough to be able to use his rifle (or machine gun) effectively. Sentries at night time were also expected to stand on this ledge. There would be various other cubby holes—places to keep trench stores, grenades and so forth. In a well ordered world (and this was a very rare occurrence) there would be another small trench leading to a latrine. The floor of the trench would have a wooden platform created by a series of duckboards, but these were often damaged and in any case under water, especially true in the Salient. A salient is a part of the line that sticks out into the enemy's line, which means one is liable to fire from three sides. There were many salients in the Great War, but only one Salient —that at Ypres.

Behind the Front line was a support line—generally a few hundred yards to the rear, and beyond this was a reserve trench. These were connected by a series of communication trenches that enabled men to move back and forward in relative security—the most famous one in this area was China Wall.

In front of the trenches was a complex tangle of barbed wire that provided a major obstacle to any would-be attacker. These barbed wire obstacles became more and more considerable and formidable as the war went on, reaching a fine art in the German Hindenburg Line. Originally there were just a few strands of wire, then knife rests were used and finally great coils supported by barbed wire screw pickets. Plenty of examples of these pickets may be observed here; they were designed to be screwed into the ground. In the early days of the war the wire was held in position by wooden pegs that had to be hammered in to the ground— understandably not a particularly popular task given the proximity of the enemy positions.

This was the theory of trench construction, the practice was usually very different; trenches collapsed because of the weather or hostile shelling. In this respect the German minenwerfer—a type of mortar—was especially feared. In times of really bad weather or enemy activity trenches disintegrated into a shadow of their former selves. When the problem of the high water table in this part of Europe was added to the list of hazards, the result was a miserable trench existence, with men standing in water and mud, with nowhere dry to rest and where more wit and wisdom was needed to ensure an at least tolerable existence than was needed to oppose the enemy.

Matters were made worse for the British by the line that they held in the Salient, as their trenches were liable to fire from the front, the sides and quite often from the rear as well.

As the war progressed and conditions in the trenches became increasingly unacceptable, there was a move towards creating strong points based on concrete emplacements, or pill boxes, some of which were very large. There are a number of pill boxes in the private part of Sanctuary Wood, on the other side of the road from the museum. This development meant that the front line could be held by fewer men, and thus reduce casualties caused by the daily wastage of the war.

A walk around the trench park will also show some shell holes of various dimensions, as well as a number of rounds. There are stacks of shell cases, as well as rounds without their fuses. The wood itself was well and truly destroyed after the events of 1916, and there is only a shattered tree or two left from the pre war time. Just off the path on the return loop back from the trenches, near the door back in to the museum, there is a line of German gravestones which date from the war years. There were large numbers of cemeteries in the area, German as well as British and French, but after the war the Germans were required to concentrate those in Flanders to far fewer sites—the ones in the Ypres area to Langemark and Menen. Thus these impressive memorials over the bodies of German soldiers would have been discarded, and have ended up here.

It is possible to buy various souvenirs and books here. Among the more unusual (and the relatively expensive) are brass shell cases which have been engraved or worked to fashion them into an ornament. A lot of this was done by the Chinese Labour Corps, a large number of whom worked in the back areas to relieve British soldiers for duty on the front. These Chinese were contracted for by the British government, usually with War Lords. Their existence does not seem to have been a particularly happy one. After the war, these labourers were used to help clear the battlefields and to create the cemeteries that are such a feature of the old British front line. Producing such souvenirs would have been a welcome supplement to their miserly incomes.

When the visitor has left the museum, the next point of interest is Sanctuary Wood Cemetery, a couple of hundred yards back down the road.

SANCTUARY WOOD CEMETERY

On approaching the cemetery from the museum there will be found a solitary, ornate stone cross just outside the cemetery limits. This is the private memorial to Lieutenant Keith Rae of the Rifle Brigade. This officer was killed in July 1915 in the German flamethrower attack on Hooge Chateau which is described elsewhere. His family erected this memorial in the grounds of the chateau, near the spot where he was last seen, as his body was lost. The last member of the Vink family who owned the chateau had the memorial moved to its present site because he could no longer guarantee its upkeep, and the Commonwealth War Graves Commission have now taken on the task.

Memorial cross to Lt Keith Rae, Rifle Brigade, who was last seen in the trenches on the east side of Hooge Crater, 30 July, 1915.

A glance at the diagram of the cemetery (a copy of which will be found inside the cemetery register in the metal box in the entrance to the cemetery) gives some clue to its history. The scattered graves between the War Stone and the Great Cross are the original burials in the cemetery, made during the war. Those along the wall are those of soldiers who were known to be buried here, but whose graves were lost in the shelling and fighting that happened after their burial. Inside the wall on the museum side and furthest from the entrance is that of a German airman, Hans Roser. This unfortunate pilot fell a victim to Lanoe Hawker, and as a consequence of his actions on that day Hawker became the first man to win the V.C. for air fighting. This combat was also the first subject of the first communique issued by the Royal Flying Corps. "On the 25th July, Capt Hawker in a Bristol Scout attacked two hostile machines; one at Paschendaele at 6pm and one over Houthulst Forest at 6.20 p.m. Both machines dived to escape. Capt Hawker then climbed to 11,000 feet and at 7 p.m. saw a hostile machine being fired at by anti-aircraft fire at about 10,000 feet over Hooge. Approaching down-sun Capt Hawker opened fire at about 100 yards range. The hostile machine burst into flames and turned upside down, the observer falling out. The machine and pilot crashed to earth south-east of Zillebeke in our lines."

It is worth emphasising the sheer danger of war flying at this time—open cockpits meant freezing temperatures whatever the time of the year; exposed fuel lines ran around the cockpit to the engine, creating a major hazard; and of course there were no

A war artist's impression of Captain Hawker's air battle 25 July, 1915. A certain amount of artistic license puts all three aircraft in the same spot, but the horrifying end of the observer is chillingly recalled.

parachutes! A bonus was that on the body of the observer was found a marked map showing the position of a number of German batteries. Hawker wrote, "..I had come on him from behind unawares—and he burst into flames and crashed into our lines. I felt very sorry for him when he fell in flames, but war is war and they have been very troublesome of late." He visited the site of the crash the next day and examined the wreck of the aircraft, also recovering the dead pilot's Iron Cross, which had been cracked by the heat. Hawker was shot down and killed by the Red Baron, Manfred von Richtofen, on 23rd November 1916 near Luisenhof Farm on the Somme. His body was lost, and he is commemorated on the walls of the RFC and RAF Memorial to the Missing in Arras.

The most notable amongst the British graves is that of Gilbert Talbot; his name has been perpetuated by the Toc H movement. He was killed in the same action as Keith Rae. A house opened by his brother, Rev Neville Talbot, in Poperinghe for soldiers to relax and escape from the war was named after his brother, and became Toc H in the army signalling parlance of the time. This house became the basis of "Tubby" Clayton's post-war Christian social movement. It is well worth the diversion to go to Poperinghe and visit the house, which is open most days of the year.When the war ended, there were one hundred and thirty seven graves in Sanctuary Wood cemetery; where did the rest come from? What happened here, as in a number of other places, was that isolated British graves were concentrated to a number of suitable cemeteries. The new road to the Canadian memorial (this road did not exist prior to the war) meant that this cemetery would be an ideal site for expansion. Therefore between 1927 and 1932 seventy-one graves were brought in from as far afield as the Belgian coastal town of Nieuport and the French village of Terdeghem—in fact from twenty four cemeteries. More staggering is the 1,781 others that were buried here in this period that were either isolated graves or of men whose bodies were discovered in this period. Sanctuary Wood was only one of several in the Salient (the list includes Bedford House and Cement House) that were kept open by the War Graves Commission to accept the remains found in the post war years.

A good view back to the British lines may be obtained by standing on the stone bench to the rear of the Cross of Sacrifice; the village of Zillebeke is off to the half left and the towers and spires of Ypres are quite clear

From here the visitor should walk (or drive) to the end of the road, past the museum, to the Canadian memorial which is somewhat misleadingly entitled "Mont Sorrel". It is taken for granted by most people that this high spot was so named on the map in 1914. It was not. Mountsorrel is a village in Leicestershire, where the Commanding Officer, Lieutenant Colonel R E Martin, of the 1/4th Leicestershire Regiment had his family home. This hill is not, in fact, Mount Sorrel—that was off to the south east; in fact this is the approximate site of Tor Top. Later on in the war there was to be a tunnel here, used for sheltering the troops.

Lt-Colonel R E Martin

Walking up to the memorial is a plaque on a large stone base indicating why the Canadians have placed a memorial here; and on the ground are arrows pointing to notable spots visible from here—which is a good explanation of why the position was considered to be so important by both sides.

By walking to the vehicle turning around point and following a path on the outside of the hedge that surrounds the memorial complex, it is possible to get an excellent view over the ground on which the events of June 1916 occurred. To the north-east, around the edge of Sanctuary Wood, were the Canadian positions, with the Germans between one hundred and two hundred yards away; once the trenches entered the wood they came much closer together. Proceeding to an easterly position, the two lines were feet apart—the German trenches were over 100 yards on the memorial side of the road that may be seen in the middle distance. Mount Sorrel was some 1200 yards away to the south west, and is visible. To the west is Maple Copse cemetery, just beyond a plantation of trees, situated at the southern extremity of what was Maple Copse. It was between there and Observatory Road that the attacking troops came on 13th June that removed the Germans from gains made here on 2nd June. The visitor should also take the opportunity of seeing how clearly (weather allowing) one can see into Ypres.

I would recommend that the visitor returns to the cafe now, gets a cup of coffee, and with some idea of what is around this vicinity, plan a route based on the various actions illustrated in this book.

THE HONOURABLE ARTILLERY COMPANY AND THE FIRST ATTACK ON BELLEWAARDE, 16th JUNE 1915

There are several points where this battleground may be observed. The visitor turns north off the Menin Road onto a narrow road. Finding this turning is relatively easy, as it is signposted by a green CWGC sign to **RE Grave, Railway Wood**. *This road is Cambridge Road, along the first part of which the British line ran on the morning of 16th June, 1915.* **Stop where convenient near Witte Poort Farm**, *a couple of hundred yards up the road on your left. Looking east, Y Wood was on your half right. Proceed along Cambridge Road; a few yards away from the farm, at right angles to the road, was the hedge that was the boundary between the Lincolns and Liverpool Scottish. Proceed until you are the far side of Railway Wood (on your right) and you will be on the site of the old Ypres-Roulers railway line. In dug-outs on this railway near the Menin Road were two British brigade HQs; up the line at the end of Railway Wood and beyond were German dug-outs.* **Return to Railway Wood** *and take the road alongside it ignoring the cacophony of noise coming from the kennels now situated there.*

Park *the car where a track joins it from the right—the track is impassable to most vehicles; a pair of boots will be handy here—and walk to the RE Grave, noting the shattered nature of the ground to the left (east) of the track. The memorial stands more or less at the position of the final British line on the 16th June; one may marvel at how the British moved at all when the Germans were in occupation here. The views of Ypres are very fine, as well as across to the left (south) towards Zillebeke. It is a sobering view of a battlefield that was hell.*

From here, **continue to follow the track** *around to the left (east); in recent years the thick wood and scrubland has been cleared, and one will find a large number of sizeable mine craters now transformed into fishing ponds. At the end of this track is Bellewaarde Farm.* **Return to your car**, *and continue along this road. On your left, beyond Railway Wood, is the scene of the heavy fighting involving the Liverpool Scottish. At a road junction, on the right, is the site of Dead Man's Bottom, where the German reserves were; it was a significant wood then.* **Proceed straight along the new road**; *almost immediately look to the right. Try not to be distracted by the Theme Park, but on the right in the middle distance is Bellewaarde Lake. You may wish to* **turn around at the next road junction** *and retrace your route, observing things this time from the German point of view (a worthwhile experience); or by taking the first right, followed by a left and a right, you will come out on the Menin Road near Clapham Junction.*

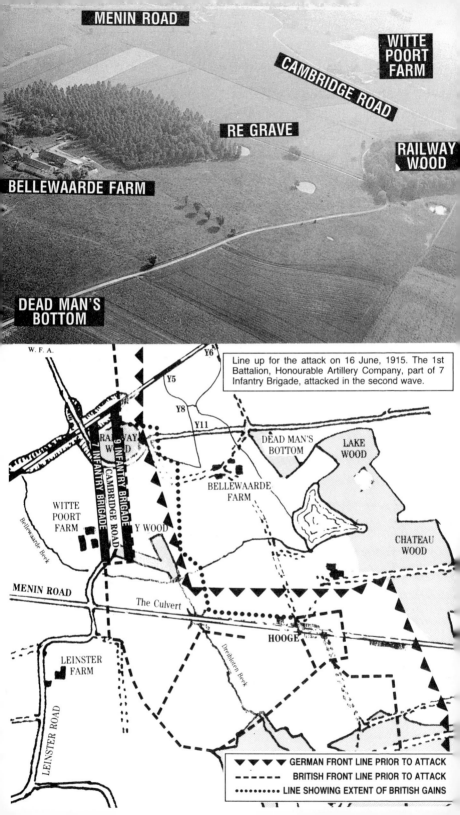

MENIN ROAD

WITTE POORT FARM

CAMBRIDGE ROAD

RE GRAVE

RAILWAY WOOD

BELLEWAARDE FARM

DEAD MAN'S BOTTOM

W. F. A.

Y6

Y5

Y8

Y11

Line up for the attack on 16 June, 1915. The 1st Battalion, Honourable Artillery Company, part of 7 Infantry Brigade, attacked in the second wave.

DEAD MAN'S BOTTOM

LAKE WOOD

RAILWAY WOOD

7 INFANTRY BRIGADE

9 INFANTRY BRIGADE

CAMBRIDGE ROAD

WITTE POORT FARM

Bellewaarde Beek

Y WOOD

BELLEWAARDE FARM

CHATEAU WOOD

MENIN ROAD

The Culvert

Dehloten Beek

HOOGE

LEINSTER FARM

LEINSTER ROAD

▼▼▼▼▼ GERMAN FRONT LINE PRIOR TO ATTACK

– – – BRITISH FRONT LINE PRIOR TO ATTACK

•••••• LINE SHOWING EXTENT OF BRITISH GAINS

The HAC is a very old military formation; its charter, from Henry VIII, dates back to 1537. It was a volunteer unit, and when the Territorial Force was formed in 1908 it was pencilled in as a battalion (the 26th) of the London Regiment; however, such was its independent spirit that it ignored this arrangement! Despite its name, it consisted of both infantry and artillery, and it recruited mainly from the well-educated and relatively well off. During the Great War it produced two infantry battalions for service abroad, and the following account, in large measure, concerns the First Battalion.

The Second Battle of Ypres had come to an end on the 25th May 1915; it had involved the first use of gas on the Western Front (by the Germans), and had resulted in a sizeable gain in ground by them, reducing the salient around Ypres considerably. The last days of the battle had been fought to gain Bellewaarde Ridge for the Germans, in which endeavour they succeeded, leaving a most uncomfortable trench line held by the British. This included Hooge Chateau, but the troops there were on the point of a very exposed salient, the British lines running sharply away south east and south west on either side of it.

On the 2nd June, after a massive bombardment, the British were ejected from the chateau—the units holding the position came chiefly from the cavalry. On the 3rd June an attempt was made to recapture the lost chateau and half-finished redoubt [strong point] being created by the British when it was lost. One observer at least was not optimistic about the outcome; Billy Congreve, a staff officer in the 3rd Division, wrote in his diary, "Arrangements are now being made to retake the chateau and unfinished redoubt tonight, but it is hopeless to try and work any scheme as long as we are mixed up with the cavalry." He commented later on, after the attack was over, "The Lincolns were sent up to help the cavalry, but the attempt failed although we did get the stables. None of us knew that the Germans had occupied the stables and, personally, I don't think they had. I knew there would be a mess up of things up there, because everyone was knocked silly by yesterday's shelling. Nobody knew where anyone else was or much about anything. Now we are going to be content for the present without the chateau and its works."

The British army was always short of shells in the early years of the war (most notoriously so at the Battle of Loos in September 1915). Yet even an idle glance by today's visitor will show the importance of the ground in this area—from Bellewaarde Ridge and the chateau at Hooge the Germans had a superb view over the British positions and obviously something had to be done to relieve the situation, regardless of the shell problem. The answer was the attack on 16th June. The situation is indicated on the map.

Machine-gun section on the Menin Road became the 'via sacra' (the sacred way) of the British Army in the four years that it fought to hold the Ypres Salient.

Shallow assembly trenches were dug in front of and behind the British Front line to enable the large number of attacking troops to have some shelter and to separate the various lines (or waves) from each other. Given the relative speed with which the operation was launched, the preparations were good—for example telephone and telegraph lines were laid in triplicate to limit the likelihood of communications being cut by hostile shelling; even a pigeon service was organised. The attack was launched at dawn, preceded by an hour and a half bombardment. The front line was easily captured, but then lack of experience in the form of impetuosity (involving amongst others the HAC) led to confusion. The second line was gained, and the third was reached, but the British were forced out of these, and further attacks failed. The line had been straightened somewhat, but at a tremendous loss of men: some 3,500 casualties.

A soldier of the HAC, H S Clapham, has given us a graphic account of the events of the days surrounding this action. He commented in his diary prior to going up to the trenches for the attack, "Everyone is suffering more or less from "wind up". It will be our first real show, and I suppose a certain amount of "wind" is natural. I certainly feel it myself, though I try not to show it." His entry on the 19th June commences, "I am quite well, but don't feel so. On the 16th we supped full of horrors, and I feel almost competent to write another story of the descent into Hell."

An artist's impression of the HAC advancing 16 June, 1915, from their positions near Cambridge Road.

The initial assault went well; the HAC was in the second line of the attack, and had to consolidate (ie improve and make defensible) the captured enemy trench. "When I dropped into the Hun trench I found it a great place, only three feet wide, and at least eight deep, and beautifully made of white sandbags, back and front. At that spot there was no sign of any damage by our shells, but a number of dead Huns lay in the bottom. There was a sniper's post just where I fell in, a comfortable little square hole, fitted with seats and shelves, bottles of beer, tinned meats, and a fine helmet on a hook."

Having moved some wire rests from one side to another, he and his party moved further down the line where a British shell had destroyed this part of the old German line. "We all started work at a feverish pace, digging out the trench and building up some sort of shelter in front. One chap, a very nice kid, was bowled over almost at once with a bullet in the groin, and lay in the trench, kicking and shrieking, while we worked." They continued working as wounded and stragglers passed back through them; they remained oblivious to what was going on further than a few yards away, with views obscured by long grass and the upward incline of the ground. Work did get interrupted. "I had just filled a sandbag and placed it on top of the parapet when I happened to glance down, and saw a slight movement in the earth between my feet. I stooped and scraped away the soil with my fingers and found what seemed to be palpitating flesh. It proved to be a man's cheek, and a few minutes work uncovered his head. I poured a little water down his throat, and two or three of us dug out the rest of him. He was undamaged except for his feet and ankles, which were a mass of pulp, and he recovered consciousness as we worked. The first thing he said was in English, "What Corps are you?" He was a big man, and told us he was forty-five and had only been a soldier two weeks. We dragged him out and laid him under the hedge. There was nothing else we could do for him. He had another drink later, but he must have died in the course of the day. I am afraid that we forgot all about him, but nothing could have lived there until evening."

After 5.30am the Germans began to shell in earnest; one "took off a sandbag from the top of the parapet and landed it on my head. It nearly broke my neck and I felt ill for some time after." The day continued. "The worst of it was the inaction. Every minute shells fell within a few yards and covered us with dust, and the smell of the explosives poisoned my mouth. All I could do was crouch against the parapet and pant for breath, expecting every moment to be my last. And this went on for hours. I began to long for the shell which would put an end to everything, but in time my nerves became almost numbed, and I lay like a log until roused." As time continued, chaos amongst the British grew, with a shortage of officers to lead, and a general lack of experience amongst the men. The Brigade-Major did a superb job—an opinion coming from several quarters—in putting together some

Artist's impression of the action which originally carried the caption, 'Over you go!' Perhaps this is how A O Pollard saw it at the time.

sort of order. At 6.0 p.m. the shelling became far worse, intermingled with gas. "I smelt gas and realised that these were gas shells. I had my respirator on in a hurry and most of our men were as quick. the others were slower and suffered for it. One man was sick all over the sandbags and another was coughing his heart up. We pulled four men out of the debris unharmed. One man was unconscious, and died of gas later. Another was hopelessly smashed up and must have got it full in the chest." A counter attack was feared; but a British counter-bombardment caught a lot of the Germans massing in Dead Man's Bottom, and it did not occur. This was not clear at the time to Clapham, who had to occupy a gap in the parapet, lying "across the body of a gigantic Hun."

With things becoming quieter, he could afford to look around a bit. "Since the morning most of the branches of the trees in the wood had gone, and many of the trunks had become mere splintered poles. Something else had changed also, and for a time I could not make out what it was. Then it suddenly flashed across my mind that the thick hedge at the back of the trench had entirely disappeared. It was right in the path of the storm of gas shells and they had carried it away." Clapham managed to leave the trench at about midnight, helping to carry a wounded man back to an aid post. "It was a rotten job, as the poor wretch started screaming, and screamed until he fainted." From here he was able (eventually) to make his way back to the rear and to the transport lines. On awakening he noted, "we have lost half the battalion and nearly all our officers, including the Colonel and the Second-in-Command. Those of us who are left look worn and old, and our nerves are in tatters. We wake up with a start, and if a shell bursts a mile away we jump out of our skins. I am inclined to curse anything and anybody. I suppose that is nerves, too."

Another soldier of the HAC present at this attack was in future to earn himself a VC. A O Pollard's book Fireater is a minor Great War classic; to my mind he appears a singularly unlikeable and arrogant man, who positively gloried in war, but there were others like him on both sides of the conflict, and his accounts are nevertheless gripping. Clapham's account shows clearly the limitations of the views of most participants in a battle as to what actually happened. He was far too busy digging, rescuing and surviving to be greatly interested in anything else that might be going on. Thus his account is of limited use as a source of what actually happened, and this is true of most soldiers in most actions throughout the war. Quite frankly they were far too preoccupied to care about grand strategy and to have an opinion about it, except for cussing the so-and-so who had put them in the position they were. Pollard at this stage in the war was a private. His reaction to the news of the forthcoming attack was a complete contrast to Clapham's. "At last! I was as excited as a girl going to her first dance. But even then I was not satisfied. We were not to make the charge but were to go over in support behind the first line. I was terribly disappointed. All the fun would be over before we reached the enemy position. At least so I thought in my ignorance...... I myself had no morbid thoughts. I simply looked upon the coming adventure in much the same way that I looked forward to an exciting game of Rugger before the War. I wanted to distinguish myself and I was determined to seize on any chance that came my way. I also wanted to christen my bayonet, although I did not see much chance of that in the second line. Roll on the hours until we move off. Let us get at them!"

Pollard was ordered to act as a link man between his battalion and the 1/ Lincolns, who were to go in to the attack just behind the first wave. It is perhaps worth noting here that the troops were issued with a new pattern smoke helmet, in addition to the primitive respirator (not bad, considering that the first gas attack had only been some six weeks earlier). This consisted of a hood made of grey flannel with a celluloid window. It was fitted over the head, the end of the hood being tucked in the neck of the tunic. To counter the gas, the hood was kept damp with chemicals, which filtered out the poisonous gases. The problems that arose included excessive heat, which meant that on occasion the choice became one of suffocation or gassing.

Pollard had an unusual view of the battle, "I had plenty of opportunity to see all that was happening. Captain Holliday employed me all day long as a runner." The early stages of the battle had gone well, and the Germans were swept aside. In a German communication trench, "I saw my first live Hun. He was lying half in and half out of a dug-out, pinned down by a beam of wood which prevented him from moving the lower part of his body. All the same he was full of fight. He had a thin face with an aquiline nose on which were perched steel rimmed glasses. He reminded me forcibly of a German master we had at my preparatory school. In his hand he held an automatic with which he took pot-shots at whoever passed him. He had killed one man and wounded one, and I arrived just in time to see a Tommy stick him with his bayonet."

After crossing the battleground, Pollard returned to his battalion and was placed with a machine-gun in the old German second line. For a variety of reasons (mainly due to the line and the lie of the land) most of the heaviest fighting took place to the north, between the railway line and Railway Wood and Bellewaarde Farm; the British were able to consolidate more easily here. "Almost immediately the Germans started a counter attack against the position slightly to our left. We could see the lines of field grey advancing and our guns got in some effective bursts of fire. Eventually the attack failed largely owing to the effectiveness of the shrapnel from our field guns."

Pollard was employed once more as a runner, and by this time the German shelling had begun in earnest, "Every gun they could bring to bear was turned on the the captured position. Shells were coming from the front, from the sides and, owing to our being at the top of the Salient, from the back." Everywhere he went in the lines he was getting names of people killed or wounded. "I began to wonder whether we should have any battalion left at all. (An officer in the Lincolns was) hit in the stomach, and although he cried out all day for water it would have been the utmost folly to have given him any. I went out and sat with him when I was unemployed. He did not know of my presence, but I felt that I was doing everything possible for him."

All this destruction began to tell on Pollard. "The day slowly passed in a tornado of the worst shelling I was ever in during the whole War. Towards five o'clock Fritz made another counter-attack and we were able to let off some of our feelings towards him in the form of rifle and machine gun fire. Any pity I had felt for any of them in the earlier part of the day was swallowed up in an intense hatred for them for what they were doing to my comrades in arms. Everywhere I went I found maimed and shattered bodies, many of them men with whom I had been laughing and joking on the previous day."

But there had to be an end. "It was two o'clock in the morning before we heard the welcome jingle of accoutrements. Followed a hail in broad Scotch. The Gordons were arriving to take our place."

The Liverpool Scottish were detailed to follow up the initial assault with the Lincolns—the Lincolns to the south and themselves to the north. They had to deal with stubborn machine-gun resistance from the area of Y6, which held up the advance in Railway Wood. However the line from Y11 to near Bellewaarde Farm was taken without too much resistance, although the German trench at this point was only a couple of feet deep, and therefore provided little protection, in particular against artillery fire. Thus far so good; but then inexperience showed and confusion set in. Some men even went so far as Dead Man's Bottom, but were never seen again.

North east of Railway Wood fighting continued for some hours in the trench network between Y8 and Y11; the enemy were assisted by a covered access to the system from the railway cutting between Y5 and Y6, from which he launched a large number of attacks in the open and also by bombing up the trench. In the end the Liverpool Scottish could not hold on to their gains on the left, because on their right the attack had never advanced as far, and the position was in grave danger of being outflanked. The battalion suffered very heavy casualties. Two officers (out of 21) and 140 men (out of 519) came out uninjured; no less than ten officers and 170 men were killed. A member of the Liverpool Scottish gave an important gift to posterity; Private Fyfe, wounded early on, took a number of photographs with his strictly prohibited camera. They are an important legacy.

Men of the Liverpool Scottish take cover, or pick their way carefully forward. Note the banner to help the British artillery spot the extent of the advance.

An Orderly Room Sergeant, J Lucy, wrote of his experiences in the battle in "There's a Devil in the Drum". He was in the 2/Royal Irish Rifles, and in the attack they were placed next to the HAC as support troops."I was busy for days before the attack copying maps of the intricate German trench system for issue to officers commanding companies and platoons." He was especially bitter about the order to resume the attack at 3.30 in the afternoon, in daylight. "The Bellewaarde Salient was now an inferno on which every British and German gun in the vicinity concentrated its fire. There was great confusion. The German front line occupied by us was filled with the dead and wounded of about eight regiments, and our men, weakened by casualties and hard manual labour, had to drop picks and shovels and go forward without direct artillery support, over muddy ground spurting shell explosions every few yards and raked by enemy machine guns from an unprotected left flank. As their waves moved forward patiently and dauntlessly to death and mutilation our officers at battalion headquarters stiffened to pale despair. The companies had just been committed when the signal came through from brigade to postpone the attack. Horror seized every one. The attack petered out, and the survivors fell back to the German front line exhausted and defeated. Our smashed battalion was relieved. Comment was impossible. Bleary-eyed, loose-lipped, and muddied, the battered men went back to rest."

The 3/Worcesters was the other battalion ordered to join in the afternoon attack. The two companies ordered forward became entangled in the confused mass of men and wounded in the captured trenches, and were then hammered by a hail of German fire, as the shattered remnants took shelter in some trees near the lake, awaiting support. This arrived in the shape of men from the 14th Division (whose memorial, incidentally, stood on the edge of Railway Wood until damage caused by subsidence of mining tunnels led to its removal to its present site at Hill 60); but men were no good against the vast superiority of the German artillery. The regimental history says, "The seven thousand troops crowded in a space not more than a thousand yards square were pounded incessantly by heavy shells: and the losses were terrible. As sunset approached the German gunners redoubled their fire, as if determined to destroy the attackers before they had a chance to reorganise under cover of night. From 7 pm till 8.15 pm the German bombardment was intense, and observers counted an average of ninety shells a minute crashing down on the Spur."

7th Brigade war diary summarised the day. "The result of these operations was the gain of 250 yards of ground on a front of 800 yards. Over two hundred prisoners and three machine-guns were taken and the enemy suffered severe losses." Yet enemy losses

A war artist captures the action that brought L/Cpl Joynson the DCM. A member of the 1st Northumberland Fusiliers he was sent forward to help the bombers of the Liverpool Scottish hold their position on 16 June.

must have been light compared to those of the attackers. Nine battalions of the 3rd Division lost just under four thousand men in an area approximately a thousand yards square. 3/Worcesters lost three hundred men, for example, though surprisingly few killed—three officers and thirty men. What did happen was a number of desertions: one just before the Hooge attack and three others (two absconding together, one separately) when warned for the trenches once more in the Hooge sector at the end of June. After court martial they were executed by separate firing squads on July 26 at the Ramparts at Ypres, and buried there. They have subsequently been buried in war grave cemeteries in the Salient.

Billy Congreve, ADC to the 3rd Division commander, General Haldane, once more provides us with a critical and observant view of a battle—this time in its aftermath. His diary entry for 19th June reads, "Around the line with the General. Interesting, but horrible—as is always the case after a big or fairly big fight. We left the Ecole about 2 p.m. and went along the railway till we came to the Gordon Farm communication trench, then to just south of Birr crossroads and up the trench towards Witt (sic) Poort Farm. It was here that the first unpleasant sights met one—a man's foot sitting all by itself made the General jump a bit. It did look rather sad. It was about here that the Germans put most of their heavy crumps, and the place was badly chewed up. From just south of the farm, we cut across to Y Wood through the assembly trenches. Half way there we found Baird, who is commanding the Gordons. He was very jumpy, and looked ill, and sitting amongst a whole lot of beastliness which nobody seemed to much worry about. We left him, as he was past reasonable conversation."

"Y Wood was in a bad state. Our bombardment must have been beastly. The big 9.2-inch and 6-inch shells had knocked all the trees endways and most of the trenches, but a good deal of these were still undamaged and were very good—deep and narrow with formidable machine-gun emplacements and very strong dug-outs. Signs of their barbed wire were few. There was a certain amount about and that was much torn up. The lyddite fumes had coloured everything bright yellow. I noticed a lot of the prisoners brought into the ramparts were bright yellow too. I think that our big howitzer shells must be as unpleasing as theirs."

"We went down to the south end of Y Wood and out along the old German communication trench towards Bellewaarde Farm, which was now converted into an excellent fire trench. It was a good sight to be able to look down into the German line that runs up towards Hooge. The first time, I think, during the war that I had looked down on a German trench, for always are they looking down on to us. Not only did we look down into the particular trench, but we also absolutely had it in enfilade [ie could shoot at it from the side]. The Wilts bombed it up just half-way before they were outbombed."

"We went on round until we arrived due west of the farm and, there, a sap ran way out to the east, at the end of which we were building a fire trench. I went down it to see how they were progressing and looked over the parapet to see where the German trenches were. I thought I saw something half way between the lines, and there was some poor fellow lying wounded. He kept on waving his hand. It was awful. I longed to go out and get him in, but of course couldn't with the General there. The men, though, promised to go and fetch him in as soon as it was dark, and that was all we could do. He must have been fifty yards from where we were. I shouted to him to tell him that we knew he was there. Perhaps he heard. He must have been lying out there for three nights.''

"Eventually we worked our way to Railway Wood. Here the mess was very bad. Also the Germans were very close, only about fifteen yards. A burial party of some sixty men arrived and got to work, so I hope that when the 14th Division takes over, things won't be quite so bad, for it's a shame to put new troops into so bad a place as that. Everything was quiet while we were up there, hardly any snipers at work in the German lines and no shelling. There is no doubt of the value of the ground gained. Looking back towards Ypres from the trench between Railway and Y Woods, one can see every bit of ground. How it is we ever moved about by daylight beats me. I suppose Mr German has too wholesome a respect for our snipers.''

"All the men were in very good spirits. Everyone of them was sporting something German, either a helmet or cap or rifle or bayonet. I wonder if any of them will ever get home.''

There were a couple of desultory attempts to improve the British line in the following weeks in this area, but the next big effort was not to occur until 25th September, 1915.

A large mine crater near Railway Wood looking towards the British start position from the old German front line.

The First Battle of Ypres lasted from 19th October to the 22nd November 1914. It marked the final fling of the German and Allied forces to outflank each other, and the failure of the Germans to break through here ensured that the war would be considerably longer than almost anyone had anticipated.

DISASTER AT HOOGE CHATEAU
OCTOBER 31st 1914

The visitor to this action might like to park in the hotel car park which is housed in the post-war Hooge Chateau ; an alternative is to park at Hooge Crater cemetery, which is on the south side of the Menin Road. The cemetery is adequately signposted, though care should be taken as the traffic does move fast along the Menin Road.

__Cross the road__ to the small road that comes off the Menin Road heading north (on the Ypres side there is a small chapel now a museum and cafe). The chapel is on the site of one of the buildings that formed part of the Island Posts (a battleground feature — see map on page 45). __Walking up the road__, within a hundred yards, on the right hand side there is a drive in to the new chateau. Bearing in mind the laws of trespass, __proceed down this drive__ (if the gate is not locked) for a few yards and note the rather pretty ornamental lilly pond; this is the site of the Hooge Crater. The late Baron de Vink landscaped the crater to make a large idyllic pool; a German bunker (of rather later vintage than the story below) is concealed in the foliage on one side. It is worth noting here that the present chateau is of a different design and in a different position to the original. The German line on this day extended northwest from the drive's junction with the road, and is partly obscured by trees and foliage. __Proceeding up the road__ (towards Bellewaarde Farm) should provide a clearer view over the British and German lines.

__Return to the Menin Road junction__. Some fifteen yards along in an easterly direction was Bull Farm, now part of the grounds of the Chateau. __Cross the Menin Road__ and return to Hooge Crater Cemetery. The bomb store referred to in the text was inside and to the right of the entrance. Note how the ground falls away here; this explains why the British were so keen to maintain their precarious hold on fragments of Hooge and the Menin Road.

In the early 1970s the area to the east of Hooge Chateau was transformed into a theme park, centred around Bellewaarde Lake. The inevitable consequence of this is that much of the ground has been altered by bulldozers, woodland removed and the whole given up to the pleasures of the present generation. Fortunately, however, it is possible to discern much that happened in the crucial area of the chateau itself, whilst some of the very bitter fighting in 1915 may be observed from the RE Grave on Bellewaarde Ridge.

**Hooge Chateau in March 1915. A shell can be seen bursting close to the building —
the first of many that would reduce it to a pile of rubble in the weeks to follow.**

In 1914 the fighting on the ground came close to the Chateau, but not actually within its grounds. However the chateau was used as a Headquarters by the staff of the Second Division, whilst the Corps Commander, Sir Douglas Haig, had his HQ a mile and a half or so down the Menin Road towards Ypres in the White Chateau. The fighting on the morning of the 31st October had centred around the village of Gheluvelt, further east along the Menin Road, and things had not gone well for the British—so much so that General Lomax, commanding 1st Division, had to call upon reserves from the 2nd Division. Having very little else that he could usefully do, he determined to report to Monro's headquarters at the chateau, and on arrival informed him that, "My line is broken".

The two generals, with various members of their staff, met in an office (a small room with a glass verandah) to discuss the situation and see what steps might be taken to ensure that the present position might be retained. The chateau had been receiving a bombardment for some time (as was the Menin road right back to Ypres, being the main route for supplies and reserves to the British front). At about 1.15 pm a few shells fell on the chateau and in its grounds. Two fell outside the chateau; but two fell in the suite of rooms being used by the staffs, and one scored a direct hit on the room used as General Monro's office. Lomax was severely wounded and died some months later (10th April 1915), whilst several staff officers were killed and a number of others wounded. General Monro was badly stunned, yet was able to continue in command. Such a turn of events would have been bad at any time, but in the circumstances of that day they could only be described as disastrous.

Thus it must have seemed to Haig, who had heard of the worsening of the gap in the Gheluvelt area, and had committed his last reserves. The news of the shell at Hooge Chateau and its effective removal of much of the staffs of two key divisions arrived at 1.50 pm. The Commander-in-Chief, Sir John French arrived at the White Chateau at about 2 pm to be told of the deteriorating situation, which would almost certainly require a further retirement along a wide front in the trickiest of circumstances—tired troops, exhausted by severe fighting, severely under-officered, greatly depleted by casualties and in unfamiliar terrain. At 2.30 pm, just after Sir John French had taken his leave to seek further French support, the news arrived of the magnificent attack of the 2/Worcestershire at Gheluvelt. This unexpected onslaught had taken the Germans completely by surprise, and forced them to retreat, at least temporarily. The situation was secured for the moment. It is worth making the point that what happened on 31st October was in no way unusual as regards the events during the

The Stables at Hooge in July 1915. The British front line ran through the the ruins.

First Battle of Ypres. This does not mean that divisional staffs got blown up regularly, but rather that the situation was often precarious and balanced on a knife's edge; command and control systems were under great strains because of the huge casualties amongst senior officers (as well as, of course, amongst the men). At the end of the fighting 1/Queen's found itself reduced to one officer and thirty two men—a battalion was, at full strength, a thousand men. Since the war had started in earnest at Mons in late August 1914, this battalion had received six drafts of reinforcements! It was the worst case in a dismal catalogue of destruction of the Regular Army, where eighteen battalions numbered under a hundred effectives at the end of the battle. What is significant is what these battalions had achieved—the halting of a massive military machine, which far outnumbered them, both in manpower and munitions. The First Battle of Ypres was won, and that victory went to the 1st Corps, commanded by Douglas Haig. But it was also a victory won by all ranks from junior officers down to Drummers—a victory of initiative, loyalty and dogged determination. Finally, it must be made clear that the British Army formed only a relatively small part of the defending force around Ypres, though they took the lion's share of the onslaught. One must not forget the contribution of the French divisions that held the line to the south and the north.

HOOGE CRATER—JULY 19th 1915

The position at Hooge was still rather unsatisfactory; the enemy still held a dominating view across the British line, which wobbled its way from Hooge along the Menin road until it turned north some four hundred yards along the way. It seemed desirable to continue operations to improve the position, and in particular to deal with a redoubt begun by the British but captured by the Germans in early June and subsequently transformed into an enclosed work which was said by German prisoners to be held by up to two hundred men.

It was determined to remove this dominating and fortified position by a strictly limited attack. A mine would be blown under it, and without any previous (and necessarily warning) barrage, it would be taken and held by 4/Middlesex.

The mine was constructed by one of the specialist tunnelling companies of the Royal Engineers, driving a shaft from Bull Farm some 190 feet long. The tunnelling was particularly difficult because of flooding—the gallery was six inches deep in water; the Germans had abandoned their own mining operations because of this problem with water. At the end of the gallery a chamber was constructed above the water level, and 3,500 pounds of ammonal

An attempt by an artist of the day to capture the horrors of a mine tunnel suddenly inundated. The Germans had ceased mining operations in the area of Hooge because of flooding problems when the British, tunneling from Bull Farm, succeeded in blowing up one of their strongpoints.

(about one and a half tons) was placed in it—at a spot calculated to be under the German work.

The mine was exploded at 7 pm. It created a hole that had a lip fifteen feet above ground level, some 120 feet wide and twenty feet deep (thus an apparent depth of thirty five feet). The trick with mine warfare was the speed at which the opposite lip of the crater was occupied by your own troops, and this the Middlesex did successfully, as the Germans were caught completely unawares. They managed to bomb their way (along with 1/Gordons) quite a way along the German trenches, but were forced back to only a few yards from the crater by the German artillery and their own shortage of bombs.

Billy Congreve (by now a GSO3—ie a staff appointment as opposed to ADC [Aide de Camp] to the Divisional Commander) reported on the attack. "The mine went off most successfully and the Middlesex took the crater without much trouble, also the piece of trench in front of Island Posts. The Middlesex worked down the trench ..., but were unable to stay there as they ran out of bombs. It was a real bombing battle. The crater is huge, and the explosion greater than we thought possible; so great that several of the storming party were burned by falling debris, in spite of the fact that they were all withdrawn south of the main road."

The conditions and difficulties of the troops in the line are wonderfully described by this dispassionate man who went on to

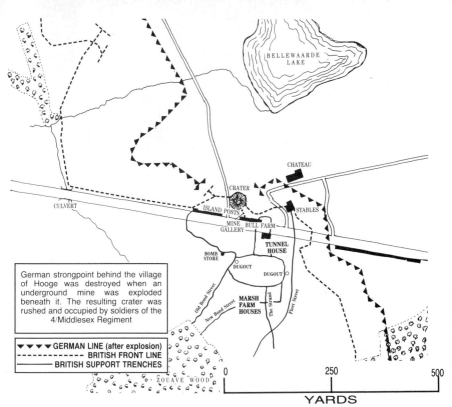

German strongpoint behind the village of Hooge was destroyed when an underground mine was exploded beneath it. The resulting crater was rushed and occupied by soldiers of the 4/Middlesex Regiment

▼ ▼ ▼ ▼ GERMAN LINE (after explosion)
------------- BRITISH FRONT LINE
——————— BRITISH SUPPORT TRENCHES

win an MC (for his work at Hooge), a DSO and ultimately a posthumous VC. He was killed on the Somme, near the village of Longueval, and is buried at Corbie. Even as a boy he obviously attracted others by his thoughtful qualities. Whilst at Eton he was ill and had to spend some time convalescing in sea air, which he did with a family friend at Lindisfarne Castle, only then recently restored by the great architect, Lutyens. So taken was the childless owner of the place, that he determined to bequeath it to Billy in his will, as he had so thoroughly enjoyed his time there. Visitors to that castle, now in the care of the National Trust, might get an added pleasure from being able to associate with such a great man. On the 21st July, he went up to Hooge once more to have a look at the situation. He describes the newly captured German trenches and the crater.

"I went down to Island Posts and, just as I arrived, the 6-inch German shells began to arrive a good deal close, and a whizz-bang knocked bricks and dust all around me. I went up the new trench into the old German trench, which one entered by crawling through a hole in the hedge. The trench was a fine strong one deep and splendid dug-outs down about six feet with at least that amount of timber and dirt on top. The best of these had already been cleared out and occupied by our men. Several of them though were still occupied by dead Germans. One had an officer in it, dead. The Middlesex must have thrown a bomb into his happy home just to keep him quiet, to judge by his unpleasing appearance.

"At the end of the trench, nearest to the crater, I had a most wonderful view of Bellewaarde Farm and Y Wood. No wonder the Germans wanted the place—it's a strong little position. To get into the crater from here was not easy, as no trench had been completed into it. However, by keeping low one could get into it at the back. It was a sight I shall never forget. The hole was huge, at least forty yards in diameter and thirty feet deep, but these figures give no idea of what the place looked like. The earth had been thrown up into a high 'lip' all round. On the north and east side of this lip, our men had made good a sandbag parapet and parados. They sat on the great lumps of earth inside the hole, smoking and laughing, while the others kept a look-out over the parapet and finishing off the two machine-gun emplacements. "From each side of the crater, one obtains a good view of the lake and the chateau. In fact it's a most commanding point and our being there must irritate the Boche."

His stay in the crater was rudely interrupted by a shell landing on the south side of the road which blew up the bomb store,

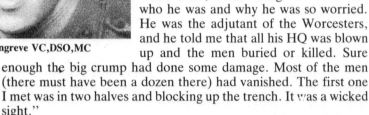
Billy Congreve VC,DSO,MC

debris from which hit Billy in the back. At first everyone thought that it was a German attack, until the cause of the uproar was ascertained.

"I went off via Bull Farm to see what had happened. The shelling was now becoming considerable, whizz-bangs in plenty and the 6-inch and 8-inch crumps all south of the road and where I had to go! I had covered some distance when I met an agitated cove who said, 'For God's sake, come along.' I asked him who he was and why he was so worried. He was the adjutant of the Worcesters, and he told me that all his HQ was blown up and the men buried or killed. Sure enough the big crump had done some damage. Most of the men (there must have been a dozen there) had vanished. The first one I met was in two halves and blocking up the trench. It was a wicked sight."

Congreve spent the next hours taking control of the situation. Men were brought out from the relative shelter of the cellars of the houses in Hooge, which had in some cases been knocked through to each other to form shelters; and there was more shelter

The Crater, developed with a parapet — there was no parados (rear wall) and this particular section of trench had to be abandoned as a fire trench. Defence was organised around the northern side of the crater with trenches dug into the lip.

for troops in the culvert running under the Menin Road. With these men he tried to restore order, despite a trying time under German shelling and minenwerfer. "This is a beast—about 12 inches in diameter and 2 foot 6 inches long, range about 700 yards. The first thing I knew about him was when I heard him coming. I looked up and saw him. He looked quite innocent. Wuff, wuff, wuff, he said. Then he suddenly steadied himself and came straight down. A moment's pause, then the most almighty big bang. Unlike a crump, there were no bits flying about—just a crash, a cloud of black smoke, and then the sky blackened with lots of things. I would sooner live with crumps than spend a few minutes with these aerial torpedoes."

The situation continued to deteriorate during the night, made worse by trying to carry out a battalion relief in the midst of all

An early post-war attempt at rehabilitation of the much fought-over ground at Hooge, next to the battered Menin Road.

the German induced havoc. Shells continued to fall. "One poor fellow had his arm blown off, and he was so hard to pick up in the narrow trench. ... All night long we kept passing men along, the double traffic being the very devil and the wounded worse."

The following morning he was able to leave the place in rather better order; whilst on the 23rd July the sector became the responsibility of the 14th Division, the 3rd side-stepping to the south to the area below and including Hill 60. Consequently Congreve's division was not in the line when the Germans launched their onslaught with flame throwers. That was to come a week or so later.

Hooge Crater today viewed from the hotel grounds, flooded and landscaped. The concrete bunker in the water is of German manufacture and dates from much later in the war.

FLAMETHROWER! LIQUID FIRE AT HOOGE
30th and 31st JULY 1915

The visitor should park at the Hooge Crater Cemetery, on the south side of the Menin Road. If it is not possible to stop here, the small road coming off the Menin road (just by a small chapel) might provide a suitable place, or the hotel car park.

The best starting point is near the **back gates to the chateau** on the small road that runs up to Bellewaarde Farm. On the road you are standing, at this point, you are more or less on the Front Line for July 1915, and both east and west from here the lines were at their closest. It was on the two sides of the crater, some two hundred yards or so in length, that the Germans used their flamethrowers. Some 150 yards to the west of the road, more or less in a direct line with the gates, were the G10 trenches that the British managed to recapture, and in which Colonel Chaplin of 9/KRRC was killed. It was also here that 2/Lt Woodroffe fought so gallantly, and which contributed to his winning the VC; he was killed to the south of the Menin Road, probably somewhere in what is now the British cemetery.

Going to the cemetery entrance, **proceed eastwards** along the Menin Road some 200 yards or so. There is a straight road running down to Sanctuary Wood, and apart from the bit near the Menin Road, this marks the approximate site of the British Front line here. Near the road the British line looped a little to the east, and the German line was here; the Germans made use of some housing on the south side of the road in their defence system, and it was known as the Wall. The British line, therefore, ran across the road hereabouts, going in a north westerly direction towards the stables and south towards Sanctuary Wood a couple of hundred yards or so on your right. Here may be seen something of the action of 7/KRRC.

On the north side of the Menin road, set back from the road, and in this vicinity is the only memorial of the fighting here at Hooge—and that is a cross dedicated to the KRRC. **Walking back** towards the cemetery from here and looking south to the wood and towards Canada Lane/Maple Avenue (marked by trees along the route) shows the open ground across which the British counter-attacked in the afternoon, as well as the path of the Germans who caught 7/KRRC in the rear in the area designated 'G3' (see map). **Walk into the cemetery** and right to the bottom: you are now at the approximate site of where the northern part of Zouave Wood stood. Looking east from this location can be seen the open ground across which counter-attacks were to be launched, more or less from their start point and the northern edge of Sanctuary Wood where the Sherwood Foresters dug the new trenches. The wood is shaped now rather as it was then.

49

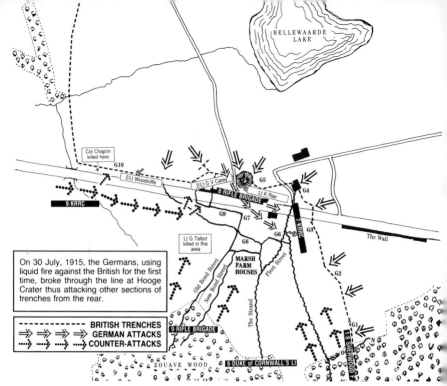

On 30 July, 1915, the Germans, using liquid fire against the British for the first time, broke through the line at Hooge Crater thus attacking other sections of trenches from the rear.

```
------------ BRITISH TRENCHES
⇒ ⇒ ⇒ ⇒ GERMAN ATTACKS
····⇢ ····⇢ ····⇢ ····⇢ COUNTER-ATTACKS
```

Hooge was where the Germans chose to launch their first attack against the British aided by the use of flamethrowers; they had used them on a number of other occasions against the French. They were highly successful at Hooge, and caused much confusion and panic amongst the British defenders. They launched their attack at the end of July 1915, with the aim of establishing control over the remaining dominant ground held by the British in the area around Hooge Chateau.

The rigorous German pressure on the British in their crater continued, making it untenable. Apologies for trenches, damaged by the incessant shell fire, ran up to the lip on either side, but with no definite connection between them around the crater (the original defence was essentially a sandwich of sandbags in which the British sat). The relief of battalions was allowed to go undisturbed, despite the extreme proximity of the trenches in places, so that bombs could have wrought great damage, especially in the confusion of the hand over. This was ominous. Stand to— the practice of all men equipping themselves with their kit and manning their posts ready to repel an attack—took place as customary half an hour before dawn. The men would expect to hold this position for an hour or so—the most vulnerable time in the trenches, when the enemy might be expected to use the tricks of light at this time to effect a surprise.

At 3.15 am the Germans launched their attack. The remnants

of the stables were blown up, whilst simultaneously men of the
8/Rifle Brigade were subject to jets of flame streaming from the
German parapets rather like water might come from a large hose.
At the same time a massive bombardment of shells and mortars,
grenades and machine-guns was opened on the communication
trenches and the three hundred yards or so of ground between the
Front Line and the Support Lines in Zouave and Sanctuary
Woods. The defenders were hustled from their trenches; but the
Germans stopped immediately to consolidate their position, and
tried to extend it eastwards by launching an all-out assault on the
7/KRRC, which unit eventually succumbed to the pressure and
surrendered most of its trenches. Further south 1/8th Sherwood
Foresters was attacked, but managed to hold on to its position to
the north of Sanctuary Wood. Counter-attacks were launched as
soon as practicable, in this case at 2.45 pm; always a feature of the
Great War, and often questioned nowadays, the purpose behind
such attacks was that the enemy should be attacked whilst he was
off balance and prevented from settling into his new position. In
this case they were partially successful, 9/KRRC regaining some
trenches; but the attack from the south failed dismally, men not
getting within 150 yards of the new German positions. One of the
casualties was Lt Gilbert Talbot, now buried at Sanctuary Wood
Cemetery. A member of 9/RB, his battalion counter-attacked
from Zouave Wood. The Battalion War Diary comments on 31st
July, "A correct casualty list is very hard to prepare without details
from the Clearing Stations and owing to many being killed and
wounded beyond reach." Talbot's company (C) attacked to the
left of the Old Bond Street communication trench. The War Diary
has him listed as 'missing believed killed'. Subsequently a note has
been added, 'Body found. Killed.' Doubtless his was one of the
many bodies recovered when the line was recaptured on 9th
August. For the moment the British licked their wounds and
planned their next move.

**Streams of liquid death spat out from the German lines on the morning of 30 July,
1915, heralding an assault on the British positions around Hooge.**

An eyewitness account of the events at the crater has been provided by a subaltern of 8/Rifle Brigade, G V Carey. He commanded the platoon that held up to the left edge of the crater; Lt Keith Rae commanded the platoon that ran from the right edge of the crater. Once the attack commenced Rae was not seen again -his memorial stands at the entrance to Sanctuary Wood Cemetery.

"I remember having a strong presentiment as I plodded up to the line that night (of 29th July) that I should never come back from it alive; in the event I was the only officer of my company (A Company) to survive the next twenty four hours." Once stand-to was ordered, Carey did the rounds of his platoon to ensure that the men were all on the alert, with their swords fixed (as the Rifle Brigade calls bayonets). He started on the right, at the crater, and was almost at the end of his platoon position, which fortunately for him was in part of the front line that was at right angles to the crater, when the attack commenced. "There was a sudden hissing sound, and a bright crimson glare over the crater turned the whole scene red. As I looked I saw three or four distinct sheets of flame—like a line of powerful fire-hoses spraying fire instead of water—shoot across my fire trench. How long this lasted it is impossible to say—probably not more than a minute; but the effect was so stupefying that, for my own part, I was utterly unable for some moments to think collectedly. I remember catching hold of a rifle with fixed sword of a man standing next to me and making (forward), when there was a terrific explosion, and almost immediately afterwards one of my men, with blood running down his face, stumbled into me, coming from the direction of the crater. He was followed by one or two others, most of them wounded. The minenwerfer had started, and such men as had survived the liquid fire were, in accordance with orders, giving the crater a wide berth. Then broke out every noise under Heaven! Minnie and bombs in our front trench, machine guns from places unseen, shrapnel over the communication trenches and the open ground between us and the support line in Zouave Wood, and high explosive on the wood and its vicinity."

Carey goes on to describe the desperate efforts to stem the tide; in particular C Company, to the right of the crater, seemed to have been almost completely obliterated very early on in the attack. One of the battalion officers distinguished himself enough to be awarded the VC. 2/Lt S Woodroffe commanded the left platoon, in the G10 trenches. The Regimental history reports, "Cut off from the remainder of the battalion and surrounded by the enemy he held off all attacks until his bomb supply was exhausted; and then extricated his company in good order. Later he led his men in a gallant counter-attack against a hail of rifle and

Men of the Rifle Brigade in a fierce struggle to hold onto the trenches in the area known as G10, under the command of 2/Lt Woodroffe.   2/Lt S Woodroffe, VC.

machine-gun fire and perished at their head, cutting a way through the wire entanglements in the open." His body was never found, and he is commemorated on the Menin Gate Memorial. 8/R.B. went into the line with twenty four officers and 745 other ranks; it lost nineteen officers and 469 other ranks killed, wounded and missing.

The 7th King's Royal Rifle Corps held the line near the stables, running south to Sanctuary Wood. The flamethrower attack was not directed specifically at them, though the position held near the stables did suffer from the extreme easterly part of the seeming wall of flame and clouds of smoke. An attack against the trenches to the south of the Menin road from the east was quickly suppressed by defensive fire, but were then subjected to very heavy machine-gun and shell fire. What did happen, though, was that the Germans who had captured the crater area now poured over the Menin road and attacked the G3 trenches in the rear and from the south. Meanwhile, further south, just above Sanctuary Wood, the Germans launched a flamethrower attack on G1 and a very exposed position—the Sap. However, the Germans who attempted to rush across the twenty yards between the trenches succumbed to the fire from the British. They tried once more with bombs, but once more failed. Meanwhile, in the complex of trenches between Zouave and Sanctuary Woods scenes of extraordinary chaos and individual initiative were taking place as bombing and counter-bombing took place, with even a spare

Pte R Hamilton, 8/Rifle Brigade, who held the line around the crater 30 July and won a DCM for continuing to fire his machine-gun. Even when his weapon was destroyed he obtained another and continued the fight. He is seen here defending the position from a German attack from the rear.

group of Royal Engineers being thrown into the fray. One can only feel sorry for the two battalions that had been relieved earlier —8/KRRC and 7/RB. 7/RB had only reached its rest billets at Vlamertinge (several kilometres to the west of Ypres) at 3.45 am; at 4.45 am it was put on the alert, and by 5.30 am they were ordered back to Ypres—tired, unwashed, not fed or rested, and probably with a clear idea of what was likely to be in store for them. 7/KRRC was eventually forced to retire back to the northern edge of the woods, having spent almost the whole day being fired at from front, back and flanks by all manner of weapons.

9/KRRC was one of the battalions brought up to help restore the situation with a counter-attack at 2.45 pm. This attack was against the advice of the Brigadier on the spot, who recognised the need for a planned and co-ordinated assault by at least a division with supporting artillery. He was over-ruled. 9/KRRC, 'being recently held in reserve was well rested, comfortably fed, and was in splendid fighting condition.' They approached along the Menin Road and attacked through the trenches held by 9/RB. Led by their commanding officer, Colonel Chaplin, they achieved their objective of the G10 trenches, up to their eastern end. "In this gallant assault the leading men were enfiladed by fire from Hooge village, when a gallant young officer (2/Lt Geen) and a few men, fired by a sudden zeal, made a desperate charge, and, closing with the enemy, were never seen again. The Colonel, in the act of directing his men to make good their success, came suddenly under machine-gun fire and fell, killed instantaneously by a shot through the head." This attack and the capture of G10 was the one bright spot of the counter-attack, launched across the open from the woods, which otherwise was a miserable failure.

Various battalions were rushed up to hold the line, amongst them the 6th Battalion the Duke of Cornwall's Light Infantry (DCLI). Their part in the holding battle was told in a letter from the adjutant, Lieutenant Blagrove (killed in action 12th August 1915), to his commanding officer, Colonel Stokoe, who had been wounded a few days earlier. The Battalion's task was to secure the front in the northern fringes of the woods, Sanctuary and Zouave. "They lined Zouave Wood and held it. They were grand, and nothing could move them. At dusk (of 30th July) the battle ended for a while. The Germans lined the high ground facing us, and completely commanded us at about 300 yards. We were really in an impossible position, but were ordered to hold on at all costs.

"At about 2 am next morning in the dark the Germans tried to bomb us out of the two trenches leading from us to them (old communication trenches). The artillery on both sides opened rapid fire, the din was awful. the Germans then used liquid fire but fortunately failed to get any into the trenches. Our men were dropping in all directions, and I am grieved to say the following officers were killed—Aston, Hulton-Sams, Challoner, Birch and the Doctor (McCallum). The only thing that will comfort you (and which does comfort those of us who survive) is that our men were glorious and, even though the Durhams fell back on our left, they held their ground. We were in this awful position all the following day—the 31st—and were crumped from three directions all the time. We had no food or water for forty-eight hours.

"One incident I must tell you. When they used some liquid fire some of C Company (whose officers and NCOs were all knocked out) broke from about thirty yards of front and fell back (small blame to them). The machine-gunners (under Sergeant Silver) who were just in the rear, yelled to them that if they did not go back to their line they would open fire on them and that the 6th Cornwall's were going to, 'bloody well stick it'. So the few men of C Company re-occupied their line of trench."

Blagrove was killed on August 12th whilst trying to rescue men from the cellars of the cloisters of St Martin's Cathedral in Ypres —men trapped by a deluge of shells. After the war the bodies of some forty soldiers were discovered in a cellar under the Cloth

Surveying damage caused to cellar billets in Ypres. A deluge of shells killed and entombed some forty men of 6/DCLI in cellars under the Cloth Hall. They were not discovered until after the war had ended.

Hall. They were men of B Company 6/DCLI, killed as a result of this bombardment.

The final account of this action is taken from the Battalion History of the Robin Hoods, the 1/7th Sherwood Foresters. They were sent to help stabilise the line in Sanctuary Wood in the late evening of 30th July. They were to take up a position in the wood preparatory to an attack the following day to recover the lost trenches. They had to dig themselves in with entrenching tools (a small combined pick and shovel arrangement that could fold and be carried on a soldier's back—fine for making a shell-scrape: useless for anything more substantial).

"It was an unusually dark night for this period of the year, and it was very difficult in the darkness to gather a clear conception of the trenches, this being entirely new ground to the Robin Hoods."

They were to occupy as much as possible of the lost trenches from the previous night. Two companies started to entrench themselves along the forward edge of the wood, but permission was later obtained to fall back some seventy yards to a better protected position, having suffered considerably from enemy fire. The Commanding Officer and escort proceeded to explore as far as possible the old front line trench (B8), reaching point X on the map, where they were warned by some wounded men of 7/KRRC lying in the trench that the Germans were behind the next traverse a little further on. The CO had some bombers and men brought up to make a block (ie build up a sandbag wall across the trench) and guard it. "On returning it was found the sap trench (marked N on the map) which when previously passed was garrisoned by a half company of the 7th KRRC had been vacated, and on making enquiries why this had been done, the CO was informed that the officer had withdrawn his men as he understood the Robin Hoods were taking over the trench." (This rather bland statement probably hides a mountain of emotions!). "This trench ... was, owing to its situation, in a very dangerous position. It was entirely a breastwork with no parados (ie it was a built up sandbag wall with no back to it), and consequently very much blocked the British rifle fire from B7 and B8 trenches. The easterly end of this trench was within a very short distance of the German line, from which the whole trench was enfiladed." Men were stationed in it (battalion bombers to the east end, and a garrison of half a company), whilst a machine-gun post was established at point O.

Whilst the Robin Hoods were digging their new trench, they were much disturbed by the cries of the wounded KRRC men left out in the wood and in no man's land; they managed to bring some wounded in and bury some of their dead. This new trench was to be the jump-off trench for the new counter-attack, which, fortunately, had been postponed. When the CO made a personal inspection of the northern edge of the wood he "was much surprised to find the front of the wood strongly protected with barbed wire entanglements with a large number of Riflemen lying dead in the wire. When, on the night of 30th July, the position on the edge of the wood was taken up by the Robin Hoods no information that barbed wire entanglements were in existence had been given; had the original orders to attack at daybreak been carried out, this wire entanglement would have been a serious obstacle and undoubtedly would have caused a very considerable number of casualties." The troops in the Sap had a very hard time,

Soldiers in the still intact Sanctuary Wood in early 1915

men being buried time and again by trench mortars.

The Battalion remained in the line, improving the trenches and generally making the position tenable. A patrol was sent out to check the old support trench and to see if it was occupied by the enemy. It was not, and this dangerous mission provided most useful information for the attack in strength launched by the British a few days later. The honour was to fall to 2/Durhams, who sent officers up to have the lie of the land and obstacles pointed out to them by the Robin Hoods. On the 5th August this Battalion took over the front line, whilst the Robin Hoods went into support. But the 2/Durhams had suffered a severe blow when coming up the line, having been severely shelled on the Poperinghe-Ypres road, losing sixty or so men, including the Second in Command, the Adjutant and one officer killed.

That highly successful attack is another story.

REVENGE—THE ATTACK ON HOOGE
9th AUGUST 1915

The viewing points for this battle are the same as for the Flamethrower Attack. It is recommended that the visitor reads through the account, and then follows the positions indicated on the map. The detailed account is given of this engagement partly because of its interest and partly because most of the battleground is clearly open to view.

After the chaos of the events of 30th and 31st July (previously described), it was decided that nothing but a carefully worked-out plan would resolve the impasse at Hooge which had existed since the German Offensive at the Second Battle of Ypres. This offensive had made Hooge the vital point of the Ypres Salient as it reached an apex here, and thus it became the focus of attention—or rather more accurately, bitter fighting—as both sides struggled to extract maximum benefit. For the British this meant a tolerable line that could be both defended and supported without excessive casualties; for the Germans it meant domination of the British lines in this sector.

One thing the British attack did achieve on 9th August; and that was the line here remained pretty well static after the battle until it was lost by the Canadians in June 1916.

There are important aspects about the battle which indicate the growing professionalism of the British Army. It is well to remember that prior to 1914 the British had a professional, Regular Army, of limited size (compared to the continental powers) whose main role was to safeguard the Empire, in the main from internal threats. A continental role for the army had been envisaged in the years running up to the war, but very much as a subsidiary, because it was anticipated—with some reason—that any major continental conflict would be short. The army had to adapt to a truly massive expansion in a very limited time; and the British were short of that most essential element in any army, a large reserve of well-trained and experienced NCOs. The ones they did have had been used up, to a great extent, in the heavy fighting in the first months of the war. Small wonder, then, that it was taking time to develop the army into an effective fighting force that could hold its own with the armies of other belligerents, who had for years been running conscription, maintained large reserves, held large scale manoeuvres and who anticipated deploying huge numbers of men in any war. This battle was a model of how an operation could be conducted; small in scale compared to later battles, nevertheless planning and inter-arm co-operation was of a high standard, and this in an action that included elements of the Regular, Territorial and New (or Kitchener) forces. Needless to say it was not all plain sailing, and errors were certainly made; but it was a competent effort. Language can disguise cost, however. There were over 2,000 casualties, most of which were caused by German bombardment on the newly won positions. That is a story true of most battles in the war, especially when superiority in artillery was not won. Contrary to the commonly held opinion, it was not the machine-gun that was the greatest killer in the Great War—it was the artillery shell.

The attack was to be carried out by the 6th Division, commanded by Billy Congreve's father ('Dads'), Major General W N Congreve, VC. Billy had appreciated the likelihood of this happening as far back as the day after the flamethrower attack on 31st July. "Everything is in a fair old muddle at Hooge. The fools have been doing those useless counter-attacks and have not only done no good at all, but their losses have apparently been very heavy. We are right back along the edge of Zouave Wood. It is devilish, really it is, all our work and trouble wasted. The whole division (ie 3 Division) is very cross."

"This afternoon I went around some of the 7th Brigade line, and an old man in the Irish Rifles asked me what all the noise had been about, so I told him, and he said: 'It's a sure thing that we shall be sent back there to clear up the mess, don't you think so, sir?' I am pretty sure he is right! I saw Dads tonight. He thinks he will have to go to Hooge. I bet one of us does, and hope it's him!" And, indeed, it was his father that got the job.

The preparation for the attack went well; when it did happen, the Germans were taken by surprise. To distract the enemy from Hooge, neighbouring divisions made all sorts of signs of preparing for an attack—signs that there was to be an Anglo-French attack on Pilkem Ridge to the north-east of Ypres; divisions along the Messines Ridge area digging jumping-off and assembly trenches, distracting German batteries on to their positions; whilst the 46th Division concentrated their artillery on Hill 60 which position gave the Germans such a commanding view over this part of the Salient.

Artillery subterfuge was used on a rather grander scale than previously—for once the attack was to be supported by unlimited shell fire in considerable contrast to the inadequate allocation for the attack on 16th June. The German positions were shelled from 3rd August onwards, at an early hour, overlapping at some point the usual stand-to; this meant that the Germans became used to a 'hate' at that time, and would not regard the assault bombardment as anything extraordinary. Before comments are made on how more appropriate this might have been than the bombardment of several days that preceded the 1916 Somme battle, it is worth drawing attention to the limited objective of the attack, the 1,000 yards of frontage compared to the miles of front on the Somme, and the involvement of only one division compared to the many on 1st July 1916. Not only did they have the support of British artillery, but several batteries of French guns were lent for the occasion, including a number of invaluable howitzers. Better though this was, one of the trench mortar batteries was using mortars that had the Napoleonic cypher on them—a rather startling contrast to the killing power of the minenwerfer!

The assault did face some problems—for example it was starting on a wider front than its objective, thus troops would be bunching as they came to the objective, with the problems that this can cause. Again, there was the problem of communication, most vitally with the artillery. As for 16th June, it was planned to raise large yellow flags on the parapet of captured trenches to indicate

Members of A Company, 2nd Durham Light Infantry, clutching rum jars to themselves — no wonder they look happy.

when an objective was taken so that fire might be amended accordingly; this had not worked then (mist and smoke of battle obscured them), and the plan was dropped. What was tried was an attempt at radio (but only between Brigade and Divisional Headquarters); it failed because the technology was just not up to battle conditions, but it was a sign that innovation was welcomed. Also to make an appearance for the first time in a battle was the tin hat; the regimental history of the 1/King's Shropshire Light Infantry records, "Before this action seven steel helmets were received, and served out for experimental purposes, being found most satisfactory." Actually, there were some problems with them, because people wearing them were in some cases mistaken for Germans.

The initial bombardment on 9th August opened at 2.45 am and lasted half an hour. Because of the varying distances on the front between the two lines of trenches (some 75 yards apart, some 500 yards), men crept out into no-man's-land as close to the bombardment as possible, whilst use of old communication trenches was made to get bombers even closer (remember the patrol of 1/7th Sherwood Foresters in the account of the Flamethrower attack, to ensure the state of one of these trenches). The battalions then advanced in as much depth of waves as possible to the attack—the 18th Brigade to the north and the 16th to the north-east (trying to minimise bunching). All went well—the leading waves were in the German front line trenches, in some cases, before the barrage lifted. The brigade boundaries coincided at the crater, where much hand-to hand fighting took place. Aerial spotting helped the British keep the enemy artillery under control (much of the artillery's work throughout the war was concentrated on destroying the enemy's artillery, and is known as counter-battery fire), and even the difficult task of erecting wire barricades on the German side was managed in daylight. True, after very heavy bombardment the line captured to the east of Hooge was vacated, but the Germans did not try to occupy it; in fact it was left unoccupied for most of the rest of the war. All in all, a very satisfactory conclusion to the train of events that had begun with another example of 'Hun frightfulness' a week or so earlier—apart, of course, from the great loss of human life.

The account that follows deals chiefly with 2/Durham Light Infantry. This was a regular battalion which had been in France since the Battle of the Aisne back in September 1914. In July 1915 it was at full establishment strength—that is 32 officers and 1,050 men—but only 180 of them had been serving with the battalion when it came out those few months earlier. The chief recent change was that of the Commanding Officer—fifty year old Lieutenant-Colonel Goring-Jones who had arrived from 1/DLI,

Report of reconnaissance of the STRAND Communication Trench.

August 4th, 1915.   G/6/12   4.55.am.
                                   5 - AUG.1915

SECRET

About 40 yards on our side of the junction of FLEET STREET and
THE STRAND, the Germans have built a barricade, two sandbags
thick, with large sandbag loophole. There was no sentry on
this barricade. At all points above our barricade our shells
have damaged the trench, and for the last 30 yards before the
junction the parapet is mostly gone.

There is a very strong barricade at the junction.
The defences are:-

1. The lower barricade already named. Presumably this is
    manned at night, though I could see no evidence of this

2. The trench is filled in, 4 yards in length, thus cutting
    off a traverse which might shelter an attacking party.

3. There is a small loophole on the left side of the barricade.
    I saw the sentry behind this loophole.

4. Three yards to the right is a large steel plate - possibly
    3 ft by 2 ft. It is so placed that a gun behind it will
    command the maximum length of trench. Presumably it
    shelters a machine gun.

5. I did not see any wire - but there may have been some.
    There is a general mix up of sandbags etc. which would
    slightly delay a rush.

6. An intensive bombardment of the junction of THE STRAND and
    FLEET STREET would be a great help to an attack. From the
    appearance of the parapet, I suspect a second machine gun
    at the left corner, covering the open field to the left of
    the communication trench.

Large steel plate.

Suspected
Machine gun.

Barrier high and in good repair.
No signs of bombardment.

Sentry's
loophole.

                              Sd. C.K.Pumphrey. Lt.
                                  10th D.L.I.

which was stationed in India. Some regarded him as a Boer War dug-out (ie too old and settled in his ways for the job); he proved his worth. Later in the war he was to command a Brigade.

The officers of 2/DLI commissioned a painting of the action at Hooge after the war—the only action of the whole of that conflict which they chose to remember in this way. It hung in the Officers' Mess until the battalion was disbanded in the 1950s; but a more significant annual event to ensure that Hooge remained in the battalion's consciousness was the Hooge Day Parade, every 9th August. This was obviously no minor skirmish so far as one battalion in a regiment was concerned.

The target for 18 Brigade (four battalions in a brigade) was to the right of the crater. Because of the narrow frontage to be attacked 2/DLI was the only battalion in the Brigade in the first wave of the attack, but they had the 2/Sherwood Foresters in close support, whose task it was to secure the eastern flank of the attack.

Before the attack was launched, details of the results of patrols were made known to platoon officers. A report on S2 (map section number) was produced by Lt. G W Rogers on 3rd August: "The Wood N. of new (Sherwood) communication trench from S3 to G1 was reconnoitred and found to contain KRRC dead along the north edge. There are several minor communication trenches at X roads south of S1 leading to S1. These were explored.

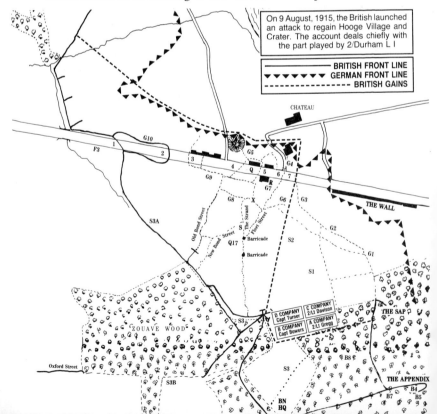

On 9 August, 1915, the British launched an attack to regain Hooge Village and Crater. The account deals chiefly with the part played by 2/Durham L I

———————— BRITISH FRONT LINE
▼ ▼ ▼ ▼ ▼ ▼ ▼ GERMAN FRONT LINE
- - - - - - - - - - - - - - - BRITISH GAINS

"S2 was then entered and examined for 21 fire bays, ie up to within about 2 bays of G6. There were no signs that the enemy had at any time entered this (S2) trench. It appeared hastily evacuated on being shelled, being hit three or four times by whizzbangs.

"S1 appeared to contain similarly no enemy.

"The Notts and Derby (ie 1/7th Sherwood Foresters) say bomb party report G1 unoccupied.

"When G6 was neared our guns were hitting S2 and G6 two traverses ahead of us, so the further reconnaisance was abandoned."

Reconnaissance of a communication trench known as the Strand the next day was carried out by Lt. C E Pumphrey; he received an MC for his efforts.

The battalion also issued comments on the ground to be covered in the attack and likely machine-gun positions:

"Trenches etc. across the Menin Road: No 5 is a trench and barricade; No 6 is a trench; No 7 is a trench with barricade.

"Points mentioned as likely to harbour MACHINE-GUNS: No 1 Junction of FLEET STREET and STRAND; No 2 Trench F1; No 3 MARSH FARM (marked S on the map); No 4 Old Trench dug-out at point marked X on map; No 5 Mound at west end of TUNNEL HOUSE (marked R on map); No 6 BULL FARM (marked Q on map)."

"There then follows a commentary on the various trenches that are likely to be encountered. "Communication trench from Crater to BULL FARM. Very shallow ground here dead to Chateau.

"G5 (from BULL FARM to STABLES). A strong parapet but poor parados.

"There is a C.T. (communications trench) across from G5 to G4, south of STABLES.

"G4 A moderate trench.

"G7 west of TUNNEL HOUSE. This tunnel is stated to be nearer to the road than the map shows it. It is described as a good fire trench with shelter trench (ie a trench with a covering of supports and earth above it) 5 yards south of it. At its east end it goes into a tunnel as do the last few yards of THE STRAND. East of the house G7 is bad.

"G8 A fire trench with T-headed firing bays facing south. Trench much knocked about.

"G6 A goodish trench, also facing south.

"S1 A very bad trench.

"S2 A good trench prepared for fire to East and wired.

"There is a communication trench connecting S2 with G1 not shown between S1 and G1. It is described as bad.

"THE STRAND was a good communication trench.

"FLEET STREET was not a good trench.

"Communication Trench immediately north and south of No 4 Barricade is practically non-existent. The ground at this point is very wet.

"Communication trench north of and parallel with G6 bad."

These reports give some idea of the quality of information that was made known to the attackers. Letters referred to a group of trenches, the numbers to a particular one or part of one; this was useful not only for the infantry, but also for the artillery, so that accurate shoots might be carried out, and speedy reference made if artillery support was required in a particular area.

After the battle was over, a full report was made out to show what had happened. This was compiled by the commanding officer as a consequence of the debrief after the action was over, and the battalion had withdrawn to rest billets.

"2.15 am. The Battalion deployed according to the diagram by 2.15 am.

A Coy 2/Lt. Gregg R.

B Coy Capt. Bowers A H M.

C Coy 2/Lt. Davison W.

D Coy Capt. Turner R V.

"The trench S2 gave the direction for the attack. Platoons deployed to single rank in distances between lines 50 yards.

"No greater distance or interval was possible because of darkness.

"The wood consisted of fully grown oak, beech, ash etc., with thick undergrowth of briar and hazel which had been wired in places. The undergrowth at the edge of the wood had been shelled away.

"The leading platoons of C and D Coys carried 120 rounds SAA (Small Arms Ammunition) and 4 sandbags per man. The 2nd line platoons carried 170 rounds SAA, 6 sandbags and one shovel per two per man.

"A and B Coys carried 220 rounds SAA, 6 sandbags and one shovel per man. (ie the weight was least for the first attacking waves, and grew progressively heavier the less likely the men involved would be in heavy initial fighting).

"M-Guns. 3 MGs were sent with the leading line, and 3 with the second line. (2 were lent with detachments from other battalions). Our 4 guns reached their destination—one gun was brought down and 3 left up on the hill when the Battn. withdrew. The latter had been buried more than once. Of these, one was out of action and was hidden in a dug-out—another could not be removed at the time but the lock and feed block was carried away.

"Bombs. Bombers of C and D Coys were to advance with their Coys and on reaching the line CRATER-STABLES-MENIN RD to push forward down communication trenches, and block them whilst the new line was being dug. 3 separate bombing parties with Lt STOREY were ordered to advance up STRAND and to proceed along BOND ST, G8, G7 where they were to join hands with the bombing parties of the KSLI (King's Shropshire Light Infantry) (16.I.B). A bombing party was sent in advance of the Battn up S2, S1 and STRAND. The bombers carried out their duties excellently, creeping forward as far as was possible under our own bombardment. They displayed activity and initiative.

"Signalling. Telephone lines were laid out before 1.30 am to previously constructed dug-outs at the southern extremities of STRAND and S2 up which signallers were sent with the leading attack platoons. These men laid duplicate lines up to the objective.

"All means of visual comm. were also arranged for but very few messages came through by this means.

"The line laid up S2 succeeded in establishing comm. at 3.45 am the instrument was broken, taken down to Bn HQ by the operator and another one taken up.

"Lines were frequently cut and mended again up till about 1 pm after which all messages were conveyed by orderlies.

"Narrative: 2.45 am artillery bombardment started.

"3.05 am Coys advanced as close as possible to the bombarded area.

"3.15 am Battn advanced to the attack. The line CRATER-STABLES-MENIN RD was reached as had been intended. Five officers were hit on the way up. The enemy held the hill in some strength with M-Guns at Q17-FLEET ST and MENIN ROAD, also at the CRATER. A staff officer estimated the number of dead Germans found around the STABLES to be 300, most of them bayoneted, and also about 200 were found in and about the CRATER.

"The 2nd Line Coys were ordered to make good G5-G7 whilst the leading companies dug themselves in on the new line.

"The bombardment appeared to be effective and the shrapnel curtain well directed (this 'curtain' was designed to stop the Germans bringing up reinforcements and break-up any counter-attacks that they might launch).

"Carrying Party. One coy. E. YORK. REGT. provided carrying parties. Each party was made to (sic) 35 men for carrying bombs, sandbags and SAA. Parties were started at 5 minute interval to carry to the dump at the top of S2—the first party started up at 3.40 am.

"3.55 am CAPT. TURNER reported he was digging in on the line ordered. He was not then in touch with 16.I.B (16th Infantry Brigade) on the left, and consequently occupied the CRATER.

"4 am. Ten prisoners reached BN HQ from Q17.

"5 am. About this time several messages asking for reinforcements were received.

"5.10 am. One coy E YORK REGT was ordered by 18 Inf Brig to reinforce.

"5.35 am. Two coys of Queens Westminster Rifles were sent up by 18.I.B but were not utilised. They occupied the trenches from which the Battn started and remained there throughout the day supplying carrying parties when asked for.

"Throughout the day it was found exceedingly difficult to send up stores. The upper portion of S2 was obliterated.

"6 am. All officers of the 2nd Line companies had been killed or wounded except Lt Sheriff—also CAPT TURNER.

"6.10 am. 2/LT DAVISON (C Coy) reported that A and B Coys had not been able to make a support trench in rear; also that the trench between the STABLES and MENIN ROAD was practically obliterated.

"At the same time LT J D CARTWRIGHT reported that D Coy was in connection with 16.I.B.

"7.30 am. On instructions from 18.I.B to thin the line to save casualties, the CO sent three messages to CAPT GODSAL who had gone to the front line to that effect. These messages were not delivered but CAPT GODSAL sent down thirty men on his own authority.

"A message sent to CAPT GODSAL ordering him to put a working party on S2 failed to reach him.

"12 noon. A message was received from CAPT GODSAL that, at 10.20 am, the front line was a continuous fire trench, in touch on both flanks, that battalions were mixed up—that there was no sign of a counter-attack—the left was on the CRATER—the right at G4 where it meets the MENIN ROAD. The front line was organised in 3 coys.

"The M.O. (Medical Officer) reported 125 men had passed through the battalion first aid post.

"2.33 pm. LT BRIGGS reported that the enemy were massing in the woods on our right front (Chateau Wood) and that the position seemed rather critical.

"2.19 pm. (sic) A report was received from OC 2/Sherwood Foresters that there was a gap of 200 yards between his left and the D.L.I. right, and stating that he would hold G6 as their former trench no longer existed.

"At the same time LT LAYNG (left company) reported that the BELLEWAARDE WOOD was full of Germans, and asking for artillery fire and reinforcements.

"2.45 pm. LT COL M D GORING-JONES handed over temporarily to MAJOR TYRWHITT, Q.W.R., and proceeded up G2 to find out the situation, taking all remaining men with him.

The CO could see no signs of a counter-attack developing and consequently returned to Battalion HQ.

"From this time until the time that orders were received to withdraw the situation remained unchanged.

"8.30 am. Two officers patrols (ie patrols led by officers) and a message in duplicate were sent up to communicate with the front line—the latter ordering the line to withdraw.

"Lt Davison (of the right company) came down with about 80 men and another party of about 40 followed shortly afterwards and reported that the ridge was clear of our troops between CRATER and MENIN RD.

"The Battn marched to billets at YPRES that night—strength 4 officers and 166 men.

"10th August 9.30 am. At about 9.30 am LTS BRIGGS, SOPWITH, WIEHE (the machine-gun officer) AND SHERIFF (left and centre companies) and about 40 men who had not received the order to retire previously were brought back from near the CRATER.

"At about 7.30 pm a party of about 24 men under No 8702 L/CPL SMITH came away from a trench near the STABLES from which they had not previously had the order to retire.

"The Germans commenced to bombard the eastern portion of the hill at about 9.30 am, 9.8.15. The bombardment increased in intensity until 11 am and was continued from that hour until dusk by means of guns from the direction of HILL 60, and trench mortars from BELLEWAARDE WOOD and FORT 13.

"Casualties on 9.8.15:
CAPT A H M BOWERS killed
CAPT R H LEGGARD killed
2/LT R GREGG killed
2/LT R W MAY killed
2/LT J D CARTWRIGHT killed
2L/T G C HOLCROFT killed
CAPT R TURNER wounded
LT G SOPWITH wounded
2/LT G M GARLAND wounded
2/LT K STOREY wounded
2/LT R K ROBSON wounded
2/LT M COVERDALE wounded
92 OR were killed and 262 wounded, whilst 100 were missing, making 466 casualties for our time in the trenches."

The Battalion had gone into the trench with some 650 men.

The Cross of Sacrifice shows the position of Hooge Crater Cemetery. The incline faced British troops as they came out of their positions at the northern edge of Sanctuary Wood.

Looking from the British trenches towards a place that became known as 'the wall' — a feature of the German front line in front of the village of Hooge.

Hooge Crater, once again in British hands, and the state it had deteriorated to by the middle of August 1915.

Private R Biggins, 2/Notts and Derbys, who won the DCM for capturing a forward German position at Hooge Crater with a small bombing party, and then holding it for 24 hours.

There are some details of how the survivors saw the operation. One anonymous letter writer described the time as follows: "At half past two in the morning (ie 9th August) we were led into a wood, and got orders to lie down, and then hell opened. Our artillery opened fire and they replied; it was simply awful, but we lay there waiting for the order to charge. It came and we lost all control of our senses and went like mad, fighting hand to hand bayoneting the hounds. I did not like to kill, but it was sport like so I did it, and wanted more. We got in to the first line and went straight on to the fourth, and past it, and then dug ourselves in under hell's flames. There were nine of us digging in the trench. I turned my back one second and when I looked again—what a sight! I will remember it till I die. Every man in the trench blown to atoms—arms, legs and heads staring you in the face. You will hardly credit what I did under the circumstances. I sat down and lit a Woodbine (a cigarette), for the simple reason I was not in my right senses. I stuck there by myself for 16 hours, and all the time a heavy bombardment of our trenches. When night came on I got out and walked back. When we were all formed, the survivors answered to their names. The old commanding officer, who is nearly seventy years of age (an exaggeration of twenty years) and a trump was crying. I can tell you we got anything we wanted. I know I got a gill (a quarter of a pint) of rum and went to sleep. When we woke up we were marched back to rest, where we are now. It was well earned."

Captain R Turner survived the war, and in 1938 he noted his

71

recollections of the attack. "I was commanding the two attacking companies; but things were so indistinct, with the dust of missiles bumping about, the half-light and the mass of trenches about, it was difficult to know when we had reached our objective. I remember prodding with my walking stick, to locate the road-way, and so get a basis for taking up our line, digging and reversing trenches etc., and preventing eager souls pressing on in to our own barrage. I got hit in the knee about this time, and in the face; but fortunately had my stick and could get along to the crater and see CSM Kent who was doing blood-curdling work. Briggs, one of our subalterns (a junior officer), (the other was hit before we moved off) was great. My leg stiffened up as it got lighter and so I could only continue sitting down, so did not get the view I should have wished of the neighbourhood. I don't think there was much of the stables left; I seem to remember a bit of an arch or gateway sticking up." Soon after this he had to make his way back to the Aid Post.

Sergeant Plews of B Company, one of those in support, wrote of the day: "Had a rum issue at 12.30 am and moved out of the wood at 1.46 and laid out on the edge of the second line to advance. We were the attacking regiment. At 2.45 am our artillery opened fire started by a 9.2 (a British howitzer) and it was a most glorious sight to see. At 3.05 am our guns lifted the range and we started the advance under a very feeble rifle fire and a little shell fire, but it increased as we got nearer the enemy's lines. A general mix-up followed of all our battalion and we advanced too far, we were under our own artillery fire and we dug ourselves in between the enemy's 2nd and 3rd lines about 5 yards off their third line. It was hell just at that time, but we very gamely stuck to it; all our company officers were either killed or wounded, only Mr Sheriff was left and a very brave man he is too."

Sergeant Plews went on to describe the rest of his day. "Held on to our position under a very heavy shell fire and at dusk things began to get very quiet and nothing doing all night. No stretcher bearers of our regiment came near us, and a very large number of wounded—poor devils. No water to be got anywhere and men crying out for it terrible. Early in the morning about 5 am on the Tuesday, the enemy were seen to be preparing for a counter attack but the artillery observer must have seen them, as our guns opened a terrific fire and must have done some serious damage to them. Again all was quiet and we were expecting to be relieved at any moment, we were properly done up. At about 11 am an officer of the West Yorks came and told us that our relief was in the communication trench or what was left of the trench and we were just preparing to leave when the enemy again started his shell fire, the first landed dead in the trench away to the right and that started it; he, the enemy, started to send them over just like rain, it was terrible, every sort of shell from a whizzbang to a 17 inch and also aerial torpedoes and bombs from the aeroplanes. We stuck it nearly a quarter of an hour and the order was given to evacuate the trench and let the relief take it over when the shelling had finished. We came out—49 NCOs and men and 3 officers— and a lot of wounded had to be left behind in the trenches. They must have been killed—it would be impossible for them to get away, poor fellows. After two or three very narrow escapes, we managed to reach the Wood, a most dissipated mob—it couldn't be called any other. After a brief spell in the Wood of about three hours, we paraded to join up with our Battalion headquarters and started to march out of the Wood at 3 pm and had just reached the outskirts when the enemy spotted us and sent some heavy stuff at us, curse him. After a bit of a struggle we managed to reach Ypres at the ramparts and stayed until 9 pm and then caught a bus at the opposite end of Ypres, near the Asylum and went back to our old billets in the wood— and poor sort of soldiers we all looked."

Sergeant Isaac Plews
B Company, 2/Durham L I
diarist of Hooge.

General W M
Congreve VC

General Congreve showed his appreciation of the work of the Durham's in a letter he wrote to the Earl of Durham dated 12th August: "Dear Lord Durham, You may like to hear how well the 2nd Battalion of your county regiment has done. On 9th August my Division attacked Hooge; your regiment was one of the attacking line. They took the hill with little loss, and accounted for all the Germans on it. They then entrenched the position and wired it, and occupied the trenches. This was all done by 8 am. From that hour on the Germans poured heavy shells all over them, and I am sorry to say caused them nearly 500 casualties. Not a man came away until the Battalion was relieved about midnight, and even then three officers and forty men (Sgt Plews among them) stayed on because they had not been relieved all that night and well into the next day, and a non-commissioned officer and thirty six men stayed another twenty-four hours longer.

Most of this time they were exposed to heavy shell-fire, the demoralizing effect of which can only be estimated by those who have seen it. I saw the Battalion after it had come back. The men were as cheery and as proud of themselves as possible, and ready to meet any number of Germans, for whom they have conceived a great contempt. I have told them that I am writing to report

Private H Langford, 1/Shropshire Light Infantry, who bombed out a party of Germans from a trench who were threatening the British position.

their fine conduct to you. From first to last they did splendidly."

Congreve was rather more candid in his own diary after his visit to the crater on 10th August. "It is a bad place altogether. Everywhere dead men, some days old and some blown to bits. You step over them in the trenches and see them wherever you look out over the trenches."

Billy Congreve noted the success of the attack with enthusiasm. "They hold a line (I think) from the crater to somewhere near Bull Farm and then down to Marsh Houses then back to Zouave Wood. This is a strong line which denies Hooge to the Boche, but I think that they will have to shove forward a bit when things get quieter. At present we do not hold the stables."

"They killed a lot of Boches during the attack. the Durhams were especially fierce owing to Hartlepool (the Zepp was it, or the cruiser shelling?). About fifty Boche were found hiding in the crater and they were all dealt with most unmercifully. Dads told a nice(?) story. He was going round some of the DLI—one old man he asked, 'How are you now?' 'I be all right thank'ee, sir. Slept foine last night, better than I did than night before.' 'Why, how was that?' 'Well, you see, I come up to a trench and in I tumbles, roight on top of two other blokes. One on 'em was dead, t'other aloive. The aloive one 'ad a great long whoite beard as long as my granfeyther's!' 'Well, what did you do then?' 'Do!'

74

Condition of a part of the communication trench known as the 'Strand' after the British bombardment prior to the attack by the Durhams.

(unutterable scorn), 'Whoi do; put 'un on the point, o' course.' Poor old white-bearded Boche!'' The reference to Hartlepool is to a shelling by German cruisers of the port (near Durham) in December 1914; in this action men of 9/DLI were killed (they were garrisoning the fortifications there) and thus have the dubious honour of being the first Kitchener men killed in action. A plaque on a wall commemorates the event.

Thus the 2/DLI had fought. Much of the ground that they had captured had to be surrendered because of its vulnerability to enfilade fire (in particular from Bellewaarde Farm and Fort 13); but on the other hand the Germans were not able to occupy it either. Their bravery and determination had been essential to ensure success for the rest of the action.

Back once again at the village of Hooge after the 'Revenge' attack of 9th August, 1915. The peppered walls of the ruined house gives some indication of the ferocity of the fighting in this sector.

Looking towards the German positions after the re-capture of Hooge. Bellewaarde Lake is just visible to the right. An inked cross indicates the corpse of a German soldier in the wire.

Much of the fighting around Hooge took place where Hooge Crater Cemetery is now positioned. Hooge Chapel can be seen behind the Cross of Sacrifice.

AN EXPENSIVE DIVERSION
25th SEPTEMBER 1915

*The visitor is recommended to park either at Hooge Crater Cemetery (signposted, on the south side of the Menin Road), on the opposite side of the road, on the small road leading up to Bellewaarde Farm, the junction of which is on the north side of the Menin Road beside Hooge chapel or in the car park of the Hooge Chateau hotel. Having parked the car, **walk westwards** along the north side of the Menin Road (ie towards Ypres). The British line ran parallel and about hundred yards to the north for the first hundred yards or so, and then went in a north westerly direction to the east end of Railway Wood. You are observing the ground across which 2/RIR (Royal Irish Rifles) attacked. After about four hundred yards you should observe a ditch carrying the Drieblotenbeek, a small stream, southwards under the road. This is the site of the culvert described by Clapham, and was used as an Aid Post during the attack.*

***Return to the car** and set off eastwards along the Menin Road. As you pass the parking spaces for the new theme park, look to your right and see Sanctuary Wood. In this area the Germans launched their attacks against the British in the B7 salient. **Proceed for about three-quarters of a mile**; on your left and right there are two quite large memorials. This is Clapham Junction. **Take the right turn** here (the memorial on this side of the road is to 18 Division). As you travel on this road, the house in the woods on the right was known as Stirling Castle (in a slightly different location and looking rather differently now to how it did in 1914). The road on which you are driving was known as Green Jacket Drive. After about a mile on this road there is a building on the right hand side, with a gated track leading up in to Sanctuary Wood. It was slightly to the east of this track (and in the wood) where the B7 position was. The German line ran more or less along the southern edge of the wood. Look to the north west, and you should observe the well tended hedge that surrounds the Canadian Memorial close to the Sanctuary Wood Museum. This trip will have given you some idea of the sheer size of Sanctuary Wood.*

Looking towards the German positions after the recapture of Hooge Crater

The greatest British offensive of the war thus far took place at Loos, a small mining village north of Arras, in conjunction with a great French offensive. Neither Sir John French, the commander of the British Expeditionary Force, nor Sir Douglas Haig, the Corps Commander for the attack, were very enthusiastic about it—mainly because of the continuing shortages of shells and suitable guns in the British army at this time. However, Kitchener overruled them, mainly on the grounds of the political expediency of being seen to give whole-hearted support to the French.

A number of diversionary, or subsidiary, attacks were launched to try and draw German reserves from the battle area; there were a couple in the region of Bois Grenier, just inside France, and yet another attack at Bellewaarde Ridge.

This was the most extensive of these attacks, and was on a frontage of about a mile from the Hooge sector to Bellewaarde Ridge. On the right, to the north and south of the Menin Road, were the seasoned campaigners of this sector, 3rd Division. Their assault was launched with the explosion of two mines; although successful south of the road, they could not get through the uncut wire and machine-gun positions to the chateau or the redoubt at the south west edge of Bellewaarde Lake. To the left the 14th Division could not capture Bellewaarde Farm, despite breaching the German line further north. At the end of the day the British were back in the trenches from which they had begun, four thousand casualties the worse off.

H S Clapham of the Honourable Artillery Company was in the line in the days before the attack, and his description of the area just to the north of the Menin Road is a clear indication of what conditions were going to be like for the assaulting troops.

"The first night we found ourselves in a trench opposite Bellewaarde Lake. The next company held the big Hooge Crater, and the others were in support behind. The ground all round was in a horrible condition, a mere waste of overlapping craters, churned and flung up in small hillocks, overlooking evil-smelling water-holes. It was strewn with bones, broken tools, burst sandbags and pieces of torn clothing. At one place in the trench someone had started to dig a recess for a latrine, but had stopped abruptly, and from the end of the cutting there hung down a discoloured trouser leg, with a shank of bone inside it and a rifle with a broken and clotted bayonet attached. The ground was strewn with corpses, and at night we went out and buried some of the nearest. One we found was garbed in the costume of a Sister of the French Red Cross, but how she came there it is difficult to understand, unless she had been buried a year ago and disinterred by an explosion. The bombardment went on all day and all night, with bursts of extraordinary energy about four or five

Hooge Crater recaptured on 10th August, 1915. It is described as being 50 yards across and littered with bits of human bodies, sandbags, firearms, ammunition and trench stores. Once again British troops are manning the trench running around the northern lip of the Crater.

The ruins of Hooge Chateau, situated some yards behind the German lines, is once again in plain view from the British positions around the Crater.

The Chateau stables were the northernmost point of the British line for much of the action that took place in the village of Hooge during the summer of 1915.

times a day. Our shrapnel burst almost above our heads, and with each explosion one could feel a blast of hot air fan one's cheek. When our guns were most energetic we were ordered to take refuge in a narrow communication trench, and there we sat or squatted for hours at a time, with nothing to see but a bit of blue sky above us and the Hun shells crashing all around. The big crater was one of the worst spots, I believe, although I was not in it myself. Four officers were killed there in one dug-out by a single shell which made a direct hit.

The battalion holding the trenches in front of Y Wood got it altogether in the neck. I saw their trenches blown sky-high again and again when we were allowed in our own front line. I was rather proud of myself on the third day. I managed a shave, and I don't know anyone else who did.

After three days in front, we spent another three days in the support trench, and I am not sure that that was not the worse of the two. It was old and dilapidated, with low parapets affording no sort of protection. It ended in a cul-de-sac, and at night I held the last traverse. In the daytime we were not allowed to use the two end traverses, as they were considered too dangerous, and we had to crowd into those farther down.

Each day two sections were ordered into a culvert under the Menin Road, which was also used as a first-aid post. I spent one day there. A stream ran through the culvert and we had to sit on our packs against the wall, without much chance of moving more than a few inches. It was a blazing hot day, and through each end of the culvert we could see the glare of the sunshine on the trees and the almost continual bursting of the shells. The Huns were using a certain amount of armour-piercing shells on the road, and if one happened to catch the road above us, we should have found ourselves like rats in a trap. All day increasing numbers of wounded were brought in, and the narrow space became more and more congested.

We were usually warned of the hours of special energy; but they always commenced a few moments too early and over and over again we were nearly caught. The last evening things were a trifle quieter, and we had an early visit from the men of the battalion who were to relieve us and who had come to inspect the position. Just before we left, one of their ration parties was paraded on the Menin Road, and was caught by a big shrapnel which laid out some score of them. When we did get away, my section was paraded at the same spot, and I wasn't sorry to move off."

2/Royal Irish Rifles had as its objective the southern half of the western shore of Bellewaarde Lake and an imaginary continuation of this 200 yards south. Its advance was, therefore, to be in a north-easterly direction (for the same reasons of constricted space as for the attack on 9th August). The final objective was only some four or five hundred yards distant. The assault was to be preceded by four mines exploding at about 4.19 am.

The Regimental History goes off in a heart-felt aside about the conditions of the ground. "The reader who does not know his Ypres can have small conception of the conditions under foot, and many suppose that, since summer was not yet over, the 'going' was fairly sound. It cannot be too often insisted upon in the accounts of battles in the Salient that even in summer, even in dry weather, the hole made by a shell was brimful of water in a very short time. In this case there had been considerable rainfall recently, which meant that, even for those who avoided stepping into shell-holes, each footstep sank inches at least into the mud of the churned ground. The so-called 'rush' of the assault was in such cases a very slow movement indeed. And here the opposing trenches were divided by 200 yards of this foul and adhesive clay."

John Lucy wrote a deeply evocative account of the action in *There's a Devil in the Drum.* He refers to the use of 2/RIR to fight in the action at Bellewaarde, "Worse still, and incredibly stupid as it may seem, our battalion was picked to attack over the very same ground as in June, and once more we tried to capture the Bellewaarde position It was said that the reason we were chosen was that we knew the ground. No psychological effect was attached to the possible reaction of men fighting on the scene of a past defeat over ground which all our officers and NCOs knew was a death trap. My feelings were indescribable as I said farewell

81

to friends I would never see again—men who knew what they were in for. I did not go forward to battle headquarters that day. My final task was to take last letters and mementoes for relations from my comrades. I would not post them until after the battle was over.

"On the morning of our attack our sappers sprang mines and the gunners put down a preliminary bombardment for an hour. Then our two leading companies went forward in the first light of dawn through mud and shell holes, and were met by machine gun fire which the guns did not subdue. They gained the German front line at great cost and those that remained went on gallantly to the German second line, where they were simply absorbed. The supporting company, stirred to anger and compassion at sight of the mechanical slaughter of their comrades in the open, rose up from the safety of their trenches without orders, and struggled forward to help. A few of them managed to get as far as the German second line. The rest were annihilated. Up to two hours after the start of the assault some of our men were seen moving about and signalling from the enemy second line of defence. After that there was no sign of them.

"Our fourth company still remained, and that was not committed. For a week afterwards I was busy reporting casualties. Most of these had occurred in the first hour of the attack, and they amounted to over three hundred, a large part of which I had to list as 'Missing, believed killed'.

"The men were officially reported as having fought like tigers once they got to grips with the Germans, yet I never saw them so sad going in to battle, or survivors look so stricken coming out. A large number got drunk the day they were relieved. Once in they fought, and more than fought, for again was witnessed the indomitable spirit of Irish soldiers breaking away from safety, without orders, to fight forward in the thick of battle beside their comrades in distress. By God, it was terrible! I know no braver men than these. A large number, perhaps the greater proportion, were Ulster men. All epics of old heroes pale before their straight forward gallantry."

In the late afternoon of the 30th September a delayed counter-attack took place in the chaos of the B7 salient. "Had we an adequate supply of bombs in the first instance the whole of the lost trenches would have been quickly and easily recaptured." Thus records the Middlesex diary. One of their officers, 2/Lt Rupert Hallowes, gained a VC.

In the 16th June attack, mention was made of pigeons as a means of communication, much favoured by General Haldane, the Divisional Commander. Experiments were tried; a pair were sent up to the loft from the line, but did not arrive. The signallers

2/Lieutenant Rupert Hallowes of the Middlesex Regiment won a VC when he inspired his men by leaping out of the trench and led a charge on the German positions.

were emphatic that they had indeed sent them off. A strong suspicion, later to be confirmed, was that if the birds had been released it was only for a short flight to the stewpot. By the time of the great attack these teething problems had been resolved. But no pigeons arrived at the loft where the General anxiously awaited information. At about 3 pm a tired-looking bird made it, and the message was brought to the general. "The General opened it, read it, crushed it in his hand, dashed it to the ground and strode away with a face like thunder. One of his staff, wondering what calamity had occurred that could bring such a cloud to the

Apex Trench at Sanctuary Wood. This was an isolated and vulnerable part of the British Line to the north of Sanctuary Wood.

Great Man's brow, carefully smoothed out the crumpled message and read—'I'm sick of carrying this bloody bird!'"

The key to understanding the failure here can be taken from 8th Infantry Brigade Diary. "It was thought that the number of guns and the ammunition allotted to them was inadequate for the attack. Three trench mortar batteries are also to take part in the bombardment, but the ammunition for these is also very limited." It goes on to say that, "it is doubtful if much damage has been done to his wire entanglements". To be fair, bangalore torpedoes, a new device, were used—these were hollow tubes of metal several feet long, which could be connected, which were stuffed with gun cotton. These could be slid under barbed wire and detonated, breaking it apart. Still, the brigade was short of items—only 15,000 bombs (for the ground here made the rifle a rather limited weapon) whilst, "the Brigade was ordered to hand over ninety pairs of wire-cutters to 7th and 9th Brigades, as none were available in Ordnance Stores for them, it being thus seen that after fourteen months of war even a sufficiency of wire cutters cannot be obtained before an action."

That is probably a bitter enough shot to have as a final comment on what was officially the Second Attack on Bellewaarde.

CANADA AT WAR
THE GERMAN ATTACK ON MOUNT SORREL JUNE 1916

*The account that follows falls into several distinct parts. To see the site of the various spots the reader is referred to the map. Continuing along Green Jacket Ride the road **comes to a fork**; by stopping here it is possible to get a good view of the German position prior to their attack on 2nd June 1916. The left-hand fork marks the approximate position of the German front line. Some three hundred yards down this road, as it bends to the left, some high ground will be seen on your half right; covered in wood now, this is the eminence known as Mount Sorrel. It is difficult to turn the car round on this road, so some travellers might be satisfied with a more distant view from the junction.*

*Taking the **right-hand fork** puts the visitor on Observatory Road. It is rather difficult today to appreciate the significance of the ridge during the war because of the woods that have regrown since then; but there is still enough open ground to give some impression. A turning on the right leads up to a farm, and there are earth works beyond it which it would seem fair to assume had something to do with Strong Point 13 and the famous two guns that were to be lost and recovered in the actions of June 1916.*

The turning to Maple Copse Cemetery is some hundred yards or so beyond the farm turning, and is signposted by a CWGC sign. The visitor is referred to the section in this book on cemeteries. There is limited parking space by the cemetery. The lie of the land here, in something of a hollow, explains why it was seen as a relatively secure point to place a Dressing Station.

*From here, follow the route indicated on the map, **back to the Menin Road** and then the Sanctuary Wood Museum road. **Stop** at a safe point several hundred yards along it, in a place where you may see Hooge and the Crater Cemetery clearly. It is not far forward from here that Private Fraser was a participant in the events that led to the capture of Hooge by the Germans on 6th June 1916.*

*The map will indicate the approximate positions of the Princess Patricia's Canadian Light Infantry (PPCLI) during their heroic defence of Sanctuary Wood; and, finally, a drive to the car park at the **Canadian Memorial** and walk around the south west side of the memorial will enable the visitor to see something of the ground over which the Royal Highlanders of Canada attacked in order to recapture their lost trenches.*

Panoramic view of Observatory Ridge taken from Maple Copse. July 1916.

The British controlled only one part of the Ypres Ridge at this time—Mount Sorrel (Hill 59) and Tor Top, a double summit known as Hill 61 and Hill 62. Although this part of the Salient was extensively wooded in 1914, progressive shelling had reduced many of the trees to stumps, and consequently vastly improved the observation the British had over a considerable part of the German positions.

The Germans had spent some time preparing for this attack, which was conducted entirely by troops already holding the line. With the massive bloodbath at Verdun reaching a decisive stage, and being well aware that something was afoot on the Somme, the Germans were unlikely to switch major resources for this diversion well away from where the vital action was taking place. That this is so is shown by the failure of the Germans to follow their initial success through; for very little stood between them and un-ravelling the whole British position before Ypres.

The attack was launched just after 1 pm on 2nd June 1916, announced by the firing of mines on the line at Mount Sorrel; the assault stretched from here to the Appendix, near Hooge, in the north part of Sanctuary Wood. They broke through from Mount Sorrel to Tor Top and captured Strong Points 11, 12 and 13 beyond them. Here they halted, coming under heavy fire from Maple Copse and Zillebeke; sending strong outposts forward, they consolidated their line. The attempt to break through at the Appendix failed, but the Canadians withdrew their men later on, in case of being outflanked from the German position in Hooge. The weakest part of the Canadian line was secured by 7 pm;

German outposts were removed between Rudkin House and Maple Copse, vital points on Observatory Ridge, a spur of high ground running west from the main Ypres ridge. The first Canadian counter-attack, timed for dawn on 3rd June failed for a variety of reasons. A re-think now took place; Haig, by now the commander of the BEF, did not want to divert resources from the Somme. On 6th June the Germans recaptured the remnants of Hooge, springing four mines under the defenders.

The decision was taken by the Canadian Corps Commander, a British officer, Lieutenant-General Sir Julian Byng (only in the job five days when the Germans launched their attack!) to concentrate on Mount Sorrel and Tor Top—Hooge could wait. He had some troops made available to him from the reserve, but what was most invaluable was the massive artillery fire power that was loaned to the Canadian Corps. He had available 218 guns for a very narrow front rather over a mile long. It included 116 eighteen-pounders—relatively light field guns—ranging up to a couple of 12-inch howitzers. It came from the Canadian Corps Heavy Artillery; the British 5th, 10th, 11th Heavy Artillery Groups, 3rd Divisional Artillery, 51st Howitzer Battery and 89th Siege Battery, and the South African 71st and 72nd Howitzer Batteries, whilst the 'heavies' of the flanking British V and XIV Corps were to help—an unusually impressive array of firepower.

Weather conditions held up the attack, but at 1.30 am on the 13th June, under the cover of smoke, after a massive preliminary bombardment of hours duration the previous day, and in torrential rain, the Germans were ejected from their gains of 2nd June.

87

Hooge was left in German hands, and the line in this sector fell back towards Birr Cross Roads, and from there south east through the west edge of Zouave Wood and the west half of Sanctuary Wood. The Germans established themselves in the approximate area of the old British front line, leaving a wide gap of up to several hundred yards before them, where only the occasional patrols entered.

The British Official History commented on these events: "The first Canadian deliberately planned attack in any force had resulted in an unqualified success."

THE RIGHT FLANK
THE DEATH OF A GENERAL

When the Germans launched their viscious preliminary bombardment of the Canadian trenches they caught in the front line the commander of the 3rd (Canadian) Division, Major-General Mercer and the commander of his right, 8 Brigade, Brigadier-General Williams. Except for a last minute change of mind, they might have caught the Corps Commander, General Byng. Byng had wanted to make a reconnaisance of his front and see how things could be improved, but had put off the visit. When asked if he wanted to go up on 2nd June, Byng replied after a considerable pause. "No. You had better go yourselves tomorrow and make your own proposals. I will come around and see them on Saturday."

The right hand battalion had a position in front of Armagh Wood; when the enemy fire came down, a German observer wrote, "The whole enemy position was a cloud of dust and dirt,

Men of the 13th Canadian Infantry Battalion consolidating a captured trench.

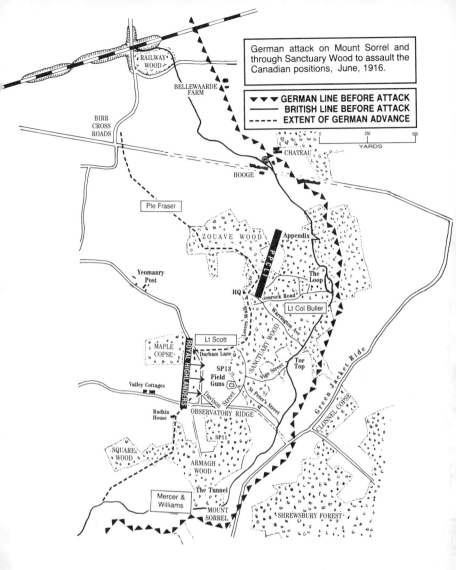

German attack on Mount Sorrel and through Sanctuary Wood to assault the Canadian positions, June, 1916.

▼ ▼ ▼ ▼ GERMAN LINE BEFORE ATTACK
——— BRITISH LINE BEFORE ATTACK
- - - - EXTENT OF GERMAN ADVANCE

RAILWAY WOOD

BELLEWAARDE FARM

BIRR CROSS ROADS

CHATEAU

HOOGE

Pte Fraser

ZOUAVE WOOD

Appendix

PPCLI

The Loop

Yeomanry Post

HQ

Gourock Road

Lt Col Buller

Warrington Ave

Lt Scott

MAPLE COPSE

Durham Lane

SANCTUARY WOOD

Tor Top

Green Jacket Ride

Valley Cottages

SP13 Field Guns

Vigo Street

St Peter's Street

Rudkin House

Davison Street

OBSERVATORY RIDGE

CLONNEL COPSE

SQUARE WOOD

SP11

ARMAGH WOOD

Mercer & Williams

The Tunnel

MOUNT SORREL

SHREWSBURY FOREST

ROYAL HIGHLANDERS

Lovers Walk

into which timber, tree trunks, weapons and equipment were continuously hurled up, and occasionally human bodies". The main shelter was in Battalion Headquarters, in 'The Tunnel', a gallery dug-out on the reverse slope of Mount Sorrel. Mercer and Williams were both wounded; both had their ear drums shattered by the shellfire. Mercer refused to stay in the aid-post—which The Tunnel had become—and decided to try and get back to his headquarters. Soon after his leg was broken by a bullet, and he was killed by shrapnel fire as he lay in a trench. General Mercer is buried in Poperinghe Old Military Cemetery. Williams was rather more fortunate—he was captured by the advancing German infantry. Of the 4th Canadian Mounted Rifles who were the defending battalion, just over ten percent made it back to relative security.

LOSING THE GUNS

The most important symbol of the spirit of an infantry battalion is its Colours—the flag that carries its regimental crest and lists its battle honours. The Royal Artillery does not have such a thing; the place of the Colours are taken by the guns.

The only time that the Canadian Artillery lost any guns during the Great War was in this action; they were to recover them during the counter-attack.

Two eighteen-pounder field guns of 5th Battery Canadian Field Artillery were in position to the rear of the front line, close to Strong Point 13, one of a series of fortified positions equipped with machine-guns, whose task it would be to limit any penetration of the front line. These were sacrifice guns, whose task it is to be placed in advanced positions to be utilized in case of emergency either for attack or defence. Consequently they are silent, till the moment arrives for special action. It is essential that they refrain from shooting if they wish to escape detection. Being so close up, an imprudent shot would at once be observed and woe to the unfortunate gunners. These gunners opened up when the attack started and kept on firing till the enemy appeared over Observatory Ridge, the hog's back running off the main Ypres Ridge. They were over-run. The German regimental history comments, "It is fitting to stress here too the Canadians did not surrender, but at their guns defended themselves with revolvers to the last man."

The forward gun position in Sanctuary Wood, captured by the Germans and recaptured by the Canadians. June 1916.

PRIVATE FRASER, 31st CANADIAN INFANTRY, AT HOOGE: 6th JUNE 1916

Private Fraser's diary is one of the finest accounts of a soldier of the Great War to emerge in recent years. He served with the Canadians until he was wounded in the Paschendaele offensive in November 1917. On the night of 5th June he went up the line towards Hooge."Along China Wall we go, continuing to Yeomanry Post, which is about three-quarters of a mile from the front line. The approaches from Zillebeke were lined with Canadian dead and further up we encountered the bodies of German skirmishers.

"We sneak into the firing trench which in many parts is shallow and blown down, on account of which the troops cram themselves into isolated spots. The 42nd Battalion, whom we relieved, beat it out quickly."

A rum jar, full of the precious liquid, was found. "To be left in the trench by such a Scottish element as the 42nd (its subtitle was 'Royal Highlanders') under existing climatic conditions is enough to upset all current theories regarding Scotsmen and the drink question." (It should be noted that Fraser was a Scot himself.)

At 7 am on 6th June the shelling became intense on the Canadian positions. Fraser comments, "Stuck in a trench, with shells gradually creeping nearer and nearer to you from the right, and through a piece of good fortune you escape, only to go through the same ordeal as the fire sweeps back from the left, is unnerving to the last degree. This systematic shellfire, which aims at the complete destruction of a helpless foe, has swelled our hospitals and asylums to the brim. No fighting is so tense as at these moments and never has reason hung on so fine a thread. To get up over the parapet and rush to certain death at the hands of machine-gunners or riflemen would be a welcome mental relief to remaining stoically in a trench with an avalanche of shells smashing and burying everything before it. Standing up to shellfire of such method and accuracy is the hardest part by far of a soldier's trials.

"It was raining continuously where my unit lay, contained only one dug-out, which sheltered an officer. The trench by this time was filled up with water, there being over a foot, and behind was a swamp. Everything became saturated with wet, the bread in the ration bags became a pulp, all eatables, except canned goods, were completely destroyed. Clothes and equipment weighed as heavy as lead. Shells were exploding all round, sending up showers of mud and water. The wounded lay where they fell on the poisonous ground of Flanders."

The attack came; the first rush was easily squashed by the

'Imperials' (British) troops on the Canadian left; but they overran the 28th Battalion, "who in the front line were wallowing in death". The 31st managed to fight them off, "notwithstanding the difficulties we were in, encumbered with the dead and wounded; the firing step smashed in many place; in mud and wet; rifles half-clogged; and though dazed and crazed we pull ourselves together, line the serviceable parts of the parapet and blaze into the advancing enemy, who recoil in confusion. All they could accomplish was to penetrate down our old communication trench into Zouave Wood."

Fraser usually worked in the transport lines, bringing up rations. He did not take part in the successful attack of 13th June. Bringing the rations up to Zillebeke, he comments: "while there stretcher after stretcher on wheels passed along the road to the dressing station, demonstrating what slaughter was going on." Later: "at night, when the fighting quietened down a bit, the dead were buried in the vicinity of the trench. A grave was dug and one of our dead was put into it, but it was too small and he was pulled out again. Some more digging and the process was repeated until finally the dimensions were made. The work was dangerous and the diggers anxious to complete their work in the shortest time and with the least labour, hence the gruesome job of fitting the grave to the corpse." One of those buried here, seventeen year old C A Owen, was not to get any peace even then. His grave was destroyed in later fighting, and his name appears on the Menin Gate Memorial.

THE PATRICIA'S SAVE THEIR COLOUR BUT LOSE THEIR COLONEL

The fighting stand of Princess Patricia's Canadian Light Infantry takes up some forty pages in their excellent Regimental history; I have extracted just two incidents.

The Patricia's was an extraordinary unit. Raised at the outbreak of War, it was to consist of veteran soldiers as far as possible. When the Battalion completed mobilization some fortnight after it was first raised, every regiment of the British regular army was represented with only one exception. The name was taken from the daughter of the then Governor-General of the Dominion of Canada: she was to become Lady Patricia Ramsey.

The Princess herself designed and worked the Colour whilst mobilization took place; whilst its staff was cut from a tree in Government House. It was to be the only Colour carried into action by a British unit during the War. Colours, under Army Standing Orders, could not be taken to the front—a symbol of the regiment of such importance to morale could not be left to the chance that it might fall into the hands of the enemy as the result of an attack. The Patricia's got around this problem because the Colour was presented as a Camp Colour only; in fact the consecration took place only two months after the Armistice! This formal moment merely confirmed what had happened after the Second Battle of Ypres (April-May 1915) when it was adopted as the Regimental Colour. Amongst other things, this meant that from then on it was always paid ceremonial honours (ie soldiers would present arms and it would be saluted). In the trenches and in battle the Colour was in the special charge of the Adjutant, and was kept at Battalion Headquarters.

What happened to the Colour here was as follows. During the German bombardment and advance, it was buried under a direct hit; those entrusted with it were all put out of action. One of the officers, Lieutenant Scott, was en route from Major Gray (now commanding the Battalion) with a message for Major-General Macdonell in Ypres. Proceeding along Lovers' Walk he came across a wounded man clutching the Colour. He assisted him to the Dressing Station. The difficult part was to come, for the Germans were in, or very close to, Maple Copse. On the journey to the safety of the Ramparts at Ypres both Scott and his runner were buried by a shell explosion and had to dig themselves out. The Colour was saved; it was the only occasion that it got sent to the rear during the War, though it did suffer battle damage from bullets and shrapnel on other occasions.

The Commanding Officer, Lieutenant-Colonel Herbert Buller, DSO, was a regular British Army Officer, formerly of the Rifle Brigade. He had made an appreciation of the ground, and reckoned that the most vital part of the line for the Patricia's to defend was their right, because of the great significance to both British and Germans of the Observatory Ridge area. Therefore he concentrated the reserves, once the attack was well under way, to the Warrington Avenue-Gourock Road group of trenches. The Germans hit hard, overpowering, eventually, the companies holding the left hand part of the line at the Loop and the Appendix, using, amongst other things, flamethrowers to help to eliminate their opponents.

Meanwhile the situation became increasingly fraught, with the threat of a German attack from any direction as the enemy broke through on several fronts. A block was built at the junction of Warrington Avenue and Gourock Road. By 2 pm Germans were seen to be proceeding along Vigo Street, which in turn connected with Davison Street and Durham Lane (and thence to Maple Copse). Thus the reserve company had to keep this threat under control (after all, the Germans might have been able to take the whole British sector here in the rear)—fortunately the number of

Germans that came this far was limited, as the enemy failed to exploit their breakthrough. The Colonel, meanwhile, was trying to defend every inch of Warrington Avenue. Eventually he decided that the only thing to do was to go forward and meet the enemy. Urging Lieutenant Scott to lead an advance up the trench, the Colonel jumped onto the parapet to get a better view, and to urge his men on. A moment or two later he was shot, and his body fell forward into the trench. The battalion was to hold the line until the night of 4th June, when they were relieved. They

Princess Patricia

brought their Colonel back and buried him beside his predecessor, Colonel Farquhar, who had died of wounds received in March 1915 at St Eloi. They are buried in one of the British cemeteries at Vormezeele, Vormezeele Enclosure Number 3, in what was then described as the Regimental cemetery. He was, the Regimental History says, idolised by his men. He had used Guards instructors to smarten up his officers and NCOs; but he also shared many of the hardships and dangers of his own men, and made a point of visiting men returned from the line to thank them and tell with obvious feeling how he had been sharing their hardships in spirit though he could not always share them in the line.

RECAPTURE: THE ROYAL HIGHLANDERS OF CANADA 13th JUNE

The task that involved this unit on 13th June may be summarised by following the orders given to the Battalion Bombers. The Battalion was to set off from a line running south to Observatory Road from the south end of Maple Copse. The dressing station was situated at Valley Cottages. Squads of the bombers were to move up Observatory Road and Vigo Street; from there, some were to put a block on the communication trench opposite St Peter's Street, whilst others were to move up Crab Crawl and Torr (sic) Top and establish a block in the communication trench opposite the latter (ie Tor Top). This would bring them to the old front line, which was codenamed 'Vancouver' for the operation.

The fighting was difficult, though the preliminary bombardment had dealt with most of the enemy wire. The further they got into the German lines, the more stiff the resistance became. Bitter hand to hand fighting, bombing and bayonetting characterised the struggle. One company commander came around a corner and, "came face to face with a large Hun. Both were surprised, but Mathewson (the company commander), recovering his wits first, planted his fist with terrific force into the Hun's jaw. The latter went down without a word, but was not altogether the loser in the contest as Mathewson's fist was badly shattered." In the area around Tor Top many of the bombers became casualties, having already lost their officer, Lieutenant Giveen (who is buried at Hooge Crater Military Cemetery), to a machine-gun some time earlier. The communication trenches forward of Torr Top had to be blocked and the new line established, which was done quickly and effectively despite the rain and the atrocious conditions under foot.

Fraser commented on the battle in his entry for 14th June: "The total operation cost the Canadians about 7,000 men. The net result was severe losses on both sides, with the Hun in possession of the ruins of Hooge. Once again (as at St Eloi) we let go a small strip of ground which the Imperials had contested bitterly. On 16th June 1915, the veteran Imperial 3rd Division, always in the van, took the Hooge Sector. A section was lost on the following 30th July by a brigade of the 14th Light Infantry Division, but was subsequently regained by the 6th Division on August 9th. Judging

Lt Colonel Buchanan, Commanding Officer, and men of 13th Canadian Infantry Battalion in a front line trench. July 1916.

by these results, therefore, the British Tommies had good cause to grouch because we did not hold the ground turned over to us and it ill befits those patriots to talk so loosely and loud about the Canadians never losing a trench. The Canadian soldier is well content to rest on his just laurels, without untruths being brought in, for the sake of placing him on a higher plane than other soldiers."

The Canadians did more than create "just laurels" as the war progressed; their corps became one of the most successful and feared formations of the war.

Canadian memorial at Mount Sorrel; subsequent to this photograph being taken the area around the memorial has been cleared of the vegetation to give clear views to the East, South and West.

THE ZILLEBEKE RAID BY
1/4th DUKE OF WELLINGTONS
JUNE 1918

The action below, small and insignificant though it was in terms of the larger picture of the War, gives a good idea of the type of large scale raids that became increasingly common in the latter years of the War.

Return to the Menin Road. **Turn left;** *within a couple of hundred yards on your left is Birr Cross Roads Cemetery. It is worthwhile to stop and look in at this cemetery. Car drivers should beware, however, of parking difficulties. In particular, it is forbidden to park on the cycle lanes that exist on either side of the Menin Road.*

At Hell Fire Corner, take the **turning for Zillebeke.** *A mile or so down the road (Cavalry Road), on the left hand side, will be found Perth (China Wall) Cemetery.* **Park here.**

To the left of the cemetery, and perhaps within the perimeter walls, was where A Company was spread out prior to the advance on Halfway House. About 100 yards from the road and the same distance from the cemetery perimeter wall was where they first encountered the Germans. Halfway House is at the end of the track that runs beside the south side of the south cemetery wall. It is about five hundred yards from the main road. On the south side of the track, close to the main road, was where the German dug-out that was bombed was situated.

On the opposite (west) side of the road is a track leading to a farm. Hill 40 is to the half right, about four hundred yards away. The site of the Moated Grange is four hundred yards away to the right of the existing buildings at the end of the track; just beyond the Grange was the British front line. Just behind Moated Grange, in the British front line, was the advanced Battalion headquarters for the attack.

Proceeding down the road *(in your car), cautiously, stop at the sign for Tuileries Cemetery. The cemetery is in the village of Zillebeke itself. It is on your right hand side. The cemetery is down a narrow passage between houses, so it is quite easy to drive past it. It is just beyond the site of the Tuilerie Chimney (this was originally a very high chimney, in which tiles were fired), and the west end of the cemetery marks the approximate site of three German machine-guns.*

Over to the left a hundred yards or so was the Tuilerie, part of the tile yards. Zillebeke Lake is behind the screen of trees and woodland to the half left.

The great German offensives of the Spring of 1918 had pushed the British back from all their hard won gains of the Third Battle of Ypres, 1917 (popularly known as the Battle of Paschendaele), and the new British line ran back from Hell Fire corner to approximately mid-way along the northern bank of Zillebeke Lake, which acted as a reservoir.

The action that is described is of a raid in strength (about half a battalion, 350 men) on the German lines. The idea behind the raid was to ensure that the Germans were not allowed to relax, to cause damage to the enemy and to capture prisoners for interrogation. The most important achievement was to afford the many newly drafted members of the battalion, officers and men the chance to take part in an action and gain experience of closing with the enemy. Because the raid was successful this latter aim was achieved.

It was planned to get the raiding platoons (twelve of them, each with very specific tasks) out in to no man's land by 11.30 pm, and to begin their advance at midnight. The artillery were to put down a barrage along the line of Leinster Road and if wind conditions were favourable, put down a smoke barrage to cover the advance, but not commence firing before 12.15 am. The forward platoons would take the first objectives and then on seeing a red flare fired by the CO of B Company, the support platoons were to advance on Halfway House. The raiders were to withdraw at 1.30 am.

The night of 19th June turned out to be very bright—remember, also, that this was June, but the move from Ypres and into position was achieved without being noticed by the enemy. At midnight, when the advance began, the moon was obscured by a cloud. Luck was on the British side.

At 12.10 am the two platoons of C Company who were detailed to hold Hill 40 bumped into a German working party before they were able to overpower the post on the Hill. Shots were exchanged, the Germans withdrew, and by the time the post was reached the German garrison had withdrawn. Proceeding fifty yards or so beyond the post, these platoons now came under heavy German fire, and could not proceed further. Although the German artillery opened fire on them at about 1 am, the men were able to hold on to the position until the time came for the withdrawal half an hour later.

Elsewhere things had gone much more smoothly. The barrage came down, silhouetted against the wall of smoke; 'it was a picture'. The German defensive fire (this would be laid on fixed lines, so that the guns were set on no-man's-land, and just had to be fired) hit no-one; by setting off fifteen minutes before the British barrage began, the raiders had gone through the German defence barrage. They did not suffer a single casualty from shell fire.

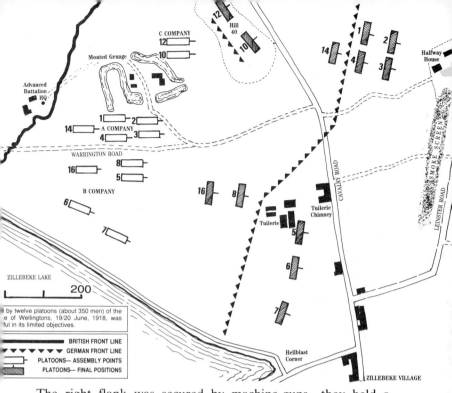

by twelve platoons (about 350 men) of the
e of Wellingtons, 19/20 June, 1918, was
ful in its limited objectives.

BRITISH FRONT LINE
GERMAN FRONT LINE
PLATOONS— ASSEMBLY POINTS
PLATOONS— FINAL POSITIONS

The right flank was secured by machine-guns—they held a
position a few yards north of Halleblast Corner (needless to say
the British had turned this into Hellblast Corner years earlier).
However, in the centre a platoon came under fire from a machine
gun post—well wired and defended—some fifty yards in front of
the Tuilerie. The wire was cut, men crept up to within ten yards,
and then rushed the position, capturing a gun and four prisoners,
though others of the garrison were able to escape. The left-most
part of B Company's attack faced a much stickier time, coming
under machine-gun fire from three guns some 150 yards from
Tuilerie Chimney; and other sections of this group came under
fire from the left. Trench mortars now joined in, and though
several attempts were made to rush the position, all that could be
done was to secure the ground held until the time came for the
withdrawal. The company commander decided that it was safe to
give the signal which would allow the bulk of A Company, on his
left and on the other side of Warrington Road, to advance. He
fired the signal at 1 am. A Company crossed Cavalry Road safely
and only made contact with the Germans once on the other side.
The Germans quickly withdrew after a couple of bombs had been
thrown; the two leading platoons occupied a line of German
trenches two hundred yards further on. Near the road a large
dug-out was found; grenades were thrown down, and three
Germans came out and were taken prisoner. The company

commander, 2/Lt Huggard, accompanied only by his runner had come well forward; on his own he rounded up four Germans who were trying to escape. A lot of the enemy were making for the rear, and were able to make good their escape in large measure because of the British protective smoke screen. By 12.45 am A Company were assembled, ready to continue towards Halfway House.

The signal was fired, as noted above, at 1 am, but became lost in the smoke and was not seen. Thus at 1.30 am the withdrawal began. Rockets were sent up from the Ramparts in Ypres to ensure that everyone had the correct direction, and white tape was laid out to guide the party back through gaps in the British wire.

At 2 am patrols were sent out to search for the wounded, the Commanding Officer himself joining in this work. Several wounded were brought in, and the work was done most effectively; at the final reckoning only one man was found to be missing. The raid had cost three killed and seventeen wounded; the patrols had captured eleven prisoners, one light machine-gun and inflicted damage on the Germans—both physically and on their morale. Two officers received the Military Cross, three NCOs the Distinguished Conduct Medal (one of them, Sergeant Loosemore, had already won the Victoria Cross in August 1917), and sixteen Other Ranks gained the Military Medal.

The Tuilerie taken by the Germans from Hill 60.

AN ENGINEER IN THE LINE
ZILLEBEKE DECEMBER 1915

*Proceed to Zillebeke. Park your car outside the church at Zillebeke, which is on the east side of the road running between the village and the Menin Road. Proceed on foot up this road on the west (opposite) side for a few yards. There is a small road leading down to Zillebeke Lake. The Brigade HQ in our account was a hundred yards or so down this road on the right hand side, a few yards short of the lake. **Returning to the church**, go in to the graveyard, and look over the rear wall to the east. The two communication trenches mentioned in the text ran to the top of the wood about a kilometre away. This wood is directly south of the site of Maple Copse. The thin belt of trees that may be seen surround the British cemetery, called Maple Copse. Gourock Road Trench was some hundred yards north, and running east in Sanctuary Wood, at the point when the visitor comes to woodland when approaching Sanctuary Wood Cemetery coming from the Menin Road.*

A working party under Sapper supervision, draining captured ground at a culvert near Zillebeke, on the Ypres-Comines Railway, 1917.

A young eighteen-year old officer in the Royal Engineers had his first experience of the front line in the trenches before Zillebeke. John Glubb was later to become a Lieutenant-General and, more notably, commander of the Arab Legion throughout the Second World War and then until 1956. He became famous as 'Glubb Pasha'. He died in 1986.

Glubb was serving with the 50th (Northumbrian) Division; but when he came into the line it was held by the 9th (Scottish)

John Glubb

Division, a Kitchener formation (ie it was a division that consisted of units that were raised as a consequence of Lord Kitchener's appeal for men) that had distinguished itself at the Battle of Loos earlier in the year. The Divisional history describes the conditions in the Sanctuary Wood sector in the winter of 1915. The 27th Brigade took over the front line trenches east of Sanctuary Wood, which at that time still presented the appearance of a wood and was full of thick undergrowth.

"All along the front line the trenches were in a very bad state and could be maintained in tolerable order only by constant labour. After a shower of rain (and it always seemed to rain in the Salient), there was the common story of dug-outs collapsed and parapets fallen in. At the best of times the trenches were ankle-deep in water; pumps were used, but they effected only a temporary improvement, because there was no place to which the water could be drained. Long thigh gum-boots were issued to the men, and these helped to keep their feet dry (in some cases they were attached to the waist to prevent them being sucked off by the mud), though they could not make them warm. In spite of whale oil and anti-frostbite grease, it is not surprising that many were evacuated to hospital suffering from trench feet (caused by standing in cold and wet conditions for hours on end). Want of sleep, perpetual cold, filth and wet were the ordinary features of life; notwithstanding the coats of goatskin that were issued it was impossible for the men to keep warm. During a man's short spell of sleep his feet became numb, and he was forced to get out of his shelter and stamp in order to restore circulation; and when he was awake he had to squelch about continually in mud, which plastered everything up to his head.

"The Sappers and Pioneers (Sappers were Royal Engineers; Pioneers were members of the battalion who had rudimentary engineering training) did their utmost to improve matters, but as regards getting rid of the water their efforts were as the labours of Sisyphus. They revetted the trenches (ie strengthened the walls with corrugated iron sheets and other supports), made dug-outs, improved and kept in repair a light railway, which was used for bringing up rations and engineering materials, but 'more could have been done if the infantry had co-operated whole-heartedly with the sappers.' Needless to say, the infantry regarded their job as bad enough without taking on another burden!"

This was the sector to which Glubb came on 14 December, when he arrived in Zillebeke.

"We are a little way way behind the front line trenches, and are badly overlooked by the Germans, both from the east of Sanctuary Wood, and from Hills 59 and 60 on the south. The village is completely in ruins. All the destroyed villages in the Ypres salient are full of horrors, with dead men and animals barely covered with earth, lying about everywhere.

"Every shattered fragment of a house is full of filth, old clothes, rags and bedding, left behind by the original inhabitants when they fled, and since used for sleeping on or torn up to dress wounds. Everything is soaked with rain, blood and dirt. Strewn around are thousands of half-empty jam or bully-beef tins, the contents putrefying, together with remains of rations, scraps of bone and meat. There is no living thing visible but rats, big brown

Zillebeke Lake at Hellblast Corner. The Brigade HQ was in the shattered building to the distant left of the photograph (which was taken in late 1917).

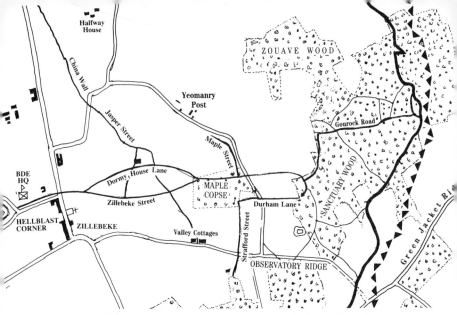

rats, who themselves are often mangy, and who barely trouble to get out of your way.

"Baker (another Royal Engineer officer) and I live in a tiny shelter about the size of a large dinner table—nine feet by twelve. It is built under the ruins of a house, which thus forms a deep layer of bricks and rubble on top of it. It is built of sandbags and corrugated iron and is only five feet high, so you have to enter almost on all fours. It is pitch dark day and night in our shelter."

He started work the next day in Sanctuary Wood. "December 16: The work on which we are employed is almost entirely repairing, rebuilding and sandbagging the trenches. The Germans shell them by day and we sappers go up and rebuild them by night. The German trenches are only twenty-five yards from our front line." (The engineers built the covered shelters that are a feature of the Trench Museum in Sanctuary Wood).

Life could be frustrating; on the 17th and 18th December he had to abandon work in the front line trenches because "the gunners wanted to have a beano on the German trenches". The two lines were so close that the British trenches had to be evacuated to ensure the safety of their own men. "All serious work is impossible in the short intervals between the strafes.

"19 December: We were woken at 5.30 am by the loud krump of a shell landing close by. Others followed in quick succession, and from 5.30 to 6.15 am, Zillebeke was plastered with shells of every calibre from field artillery to about nine inch. At the same time, there was a beastly smell of gas, and we were all weeping at the eyes. I dodged out of our shelter and ran along to check the men's shelters, but none had been hit.

"There was a battery of our field gunners just behind us, who started up also, and the noise was indescribable. Peeping out of our dug-out, I could see the Boche krumps bursting one after the other in Zillebeke Street communication trench. At about 6.15, the Boche lengthened his range and we could see the bursts above Brigade Headquarters and Zillebeke Lake.

"I went up at night with my section to repair Gourock Road Trench, which had been damaged by shellfire. We were badly shelled by 'whizz-bangs'. Ceased work early, as it was almost impossible to do anything owing to the shelling.

"Sanctuary Wood is connected to Zillebeke village by a long communication trench called Zillebeke Street. When we knocked off work, and came out of Maple Copse, a lot of heavy krumps were falling on Zillebeke Street. I accordingly sent the sappers back by Dormy House Lane. I went on down Zillebeke Street. I found a man of the Durham Light Infantry lying in the trench with a broken thigh.

"I and Sergeant Frankenburg, two sappers and a DLI sergeant carried the man to the dressing station in Maple Copse. The poor fellow's thigh was smashed and he suffered agony with every movement. He kept crying 'No! No! I can't! O God, leave me alone!'"

The next day he went for a tour of the trenches with his commanding officer and the CO of the 6th Durhams. "We were standing in the front line trench, when a whizz-bang burst in the middle of the group. Obviously sniping. They probably saw Colonel Jeffreys (of 6/Durhams), who is a very tall man.

"The shell killed three men instantly. I heard someone say, 'Are you hit, sir?' and Colonel Jeffreys answer, 'I am afraid I am.' Symons, my own OC, was lying on the floor of the trench with a wound in his thigh. I ran down the trench to get stretcher bearers, and had Symons carried to the dressing station in Maple

Photographed from Hellblast Corner, on the edge of Zillebeke Lake. Mount Sorrel looms above Sanctuary Wood.

Copse. Poor old man! We shall not get such a good OC again, I am afraid.

The Boches have been whizz-banging for two days, and the dressing station, a dug-out in Maple Copse, was crammed with wounded. The doctor dressed Symon's wound, which seemed to be a nasty one. One poor devil there had had his arm taken clean off at the shoulder by a direct hit from a whizz-bang. He was talking cheerfully. 'Those bloody guns haven't stopped for forty-eight hours,' he said."

Only then did Glubb notice his own problems. "My left foot had felt numb since the shell burst, but I had been too preoccupied to notice it much. Now I looked down at it and saw that there was a gash in my gumboot and that blood was coming out. I asked the doctor to have a look at it, and he cut off my boot, and told me that my big toe was smashed up and must have been hit by a shell fragment. He tied it up and gave me a tetanus injection. I hobbled back down Zillebeke Street to our dug-out."

It was to prove the end of his first short encounter with the trenches, as he was forced to go down the line to a Casualty Clearing Station at Hazebrouk. Casualty Clearing Stations were an intermediary stage of medical care: soldiers would normally go

Carrying wounded down from Maple Copse, near Hooge, August 1915. 18th Field Ambulance, 6th Division.

from an Aid Post to a Dressing Station, both in the front line area of trenches; from there to a Casualty Clearing Station, well back from the line; if necessary from there to a Base Hospital; and if circumstance required—such as serious injuries or a long term problem—casualties were sent to England, known to the Tommies as Blighty. Hence the desire of many soldiers to get a 'blighty one' ie a wound serious enough to get him sent home.

*This concludes the tour of the Sanctuary Wood area. On returning to your car, proceed further into Zillebeke, past the church and take the **right hand turn**. Having crossed the railway line, **turn right**: you are now travelling along a road that was always under heavy German shellfire from the south, the east and on occasion from the north as well. After some time the railway line is crossed again, and a few hundred yards further on is a large British cemetery, Railway Dugouts (Transport Farm). A large number of the Canadian casualties from the June 1916 battles are buried here. It is a place of some importance to myself, because my grandfather and the rest of his battalion (7th Leicesters) held the line here in 1918 during the German Lys Offensive. Many of the troops holding the line in the southern part of the Sanctuary Wood area came up to the line this way, proceeding to Zillebeke and then along one or other of the communication trenches to Maple Copse and then to the front line.*

*The end of this road brings the traveller to a cross roads, known during the war as Shrapnel Corner. To return to Ypres, **turn right**, and enter the town under the Lille Gate. Looking to the left a hundred yards or so before the gate, you will see the Ramparts Cemetery, to my mind one of the most beautifully situated on the western Front. I know that this was the view of Rose Coombs, to whom this book is dedicated.*

"Whizzbang" 6 DLI Trench Monthly

Clearing the ground around Hooge Crater Cemetery

In the area covered in this guide there are seven Commonwealth War Grave Cemeteries or memorials. The one at Sanctuary Wood has been discussed in the section on this wood. The cemeteries are described (briefly) in the order in which the visitor will reach them assuming that the recommended route is followed.

R E GRAVE, RAILWAY WOOD

This grave consists of a War Cross in its own enclosure, with the names of fourteen soldiers (eight members of the Royal Engineers and four attached infantrymen) engraved on its base. These soldiers were all killed underground, working with 177th Tunnelling Company, Royal Engineers. There is no register here because the number commemorated is so small— but details of those buried (in this case 'many feet below the surface') may be found in the register at Birr Cross Roads Cemetery.

The grave is in a spot that offers excellent views over the ground of successive British attacks in 1915; of Ypres; and to the south Sanctuary Wood and area. In the vicinity there are plenty of signs of the mine warfare that was such a feature of the fighting in this sector.

HOOGE CRATER CEMETERY

Hooge Crater cemetery, like many cemeteries in the Salient, was begun as a cemetery during the war (in this case in October 1917 by the 7th Division Burial Officer) and was then extended after the Armistice by the concentration of graves from smaller or inaccessible cemeteries, and by the bodies of men found in subsequent years on the battlefields. In this cemetery the majority—over sixty percent—are unidentified.

The cemetery is built on ground that saw heavy fighting in 1915 and 1916; the Bond Street communication trenches ran through or alongside it. Amongst those buried here is a winner of the Victoria Cross, Private Patrick Bugden of the 31st Battalion Australian Infantry who won his medal posthumously in September 1917. The citations of those who won the Victoria Cross is usually included in the relevant cemetery register under the name of the recipient.

Maple Copse Cemetery looking East. Sanctuary Wood in the distance

MAPLE COPSE CEMETERY

Maple Copse cemetery was established close to the Dressing Station which was at the edge of the copse of that name. The copse now is to the south of the original, which was directly to the north and west of the cemetery. Most of those buried in this cemetery had their graves destroyed in later fighting, but are commemorated here.

The cemetery is in a particularly quiet and beautiful part of the Salient. In recent years the area around Ypres has become increasingly busy, with new roads and a great number of new, small industial units. Maple Copse, situated in fields, is an excellent place to stop and enjoy rural tranquility. There are good views across to Sanctuary Wood. This is an ideal place to halt a while and perhaps to consider the enormity of the events that took place in this small corner of Europe so many years ago.

110

9.2 inch battery of howitzers at Birr Cross Roads, Ypres, during October 1917, toward the close of the Third Battle of Ypres. The artillery, owing to the weight of the guns, suffered especially in the seas of mud.

BIRR CROSS ROADS CEMETERY

The cemetery got its name from 1st Leinsters, whose depot was at Birr. Originally the Cambridge Road connection with the Menin Road was a cross-roads, but the southerly road has moved to the west since the war. The cemetery was begun in August 1917 as a Dressing Station cemetery for the Battle of the Menin Road and from then until the end of the war. The nine irregular rows of graves in Plot 1 are the original pre-armistice burials (Plot 1 is situated between the War Stone and the Great Cross). The number of bodies concentrated here in the post war years is 666, including amongst them Captain H Ackroyd, VC, MC of the Royal Army Medical Corps. He won a posthumous VC for his bravery on 31st July/1st August 1917 whilst attached to the 6th Royal Berkshire Regiment. He has a Special Memorial because he was believed to be buried with a group of men, most of whom are among the 336 unnamed graves.

Perth (China Wall) Cemetery on left. The road leads to Halfway House. To the right of the photograph was the site of a large German fortification. (See The Zillebeke Raid)

PERTH CEMETERY (CHINA WALL)

This cemetery was begun by French troops in November 1914, during the First Battle of Ypres. It was adopted by the 2nd Scottish Rifles in June 1917. It is not known where the name Perth came from; China Wall was a main communication trench from the Menin Road to the front to the south of the Menin Road. It was also known as Halfway House Cemetery, after the farm of that name which is to the east of the cemetery. It was used as a front line burial area until October 1917, when some 170 men were intered there; after the armistice over 2,500 men were concentrated here. The French plot (enlarged after the armistice as well) with its 158 men was removed in the post war years (probably to the St Charles Cemetery near Potijze). Again, a large number of those buried here are unknown.

There are two winners of the Victoria Cross buried in this cemetery. 2/Lt Frederick Birks VC, MM of the 6th Battalion Australian Infantry who was killed winning his award on 21st September 1917. He was born in Wales. Major W H Johnston VC, Royal Engineers, won his medal for great bravery in working rafts at a river crossing under heavy fire in the early days of the war.

Tuileries British Cemetery. The German machine guns were in the vicinity of the bottom end of the cemetery. To the left, middle distance, is the line of trees marking the edge of Zillebeke Lake.

TUILERIES BRITISH CEMETERY

This cemetery, tucked away behind some houses in Zillebeke. was situated in part of the tile works (the tuileries) that stood here in pre-war years. It was used in 1915, when 106 British soldiers (and a few Frenchmen, subsequently removed) were buried here. The chimney of the Tuileries was a natural ranging mark for German artillery, and the cemetery was badly damaged by the shelling. This explains the strange arrangement of the cemetery, with a large number of stones close to the boundary walls—these commemorate the 69 known and eleven unknown men whose graves were destroyed by this shelling.

ZILLEBEKE CHURCHYARD

This churchyard cemetery is also known as the Aristocrats Cemetery. More details about a number of those buried here may be found in my book 'Battleground Europe'. It is somewhat unusual to have a whole plot of a churchyard devoted to a war cemetery. Most of those buried here—fourteen of them—belonged to the Foot Guards or the Household Cavalry and fell in 1914.

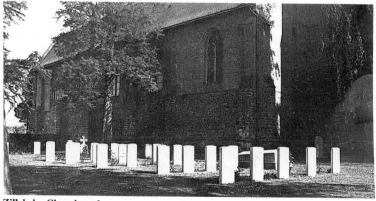

Zillebeke Churchyard

These cemeteries are maintained by the Commonwealth War Graves Commission, whose origins and development make a fascinating, and to me at least, a rather British story. No visitor can go away unimpressed with the care and the dignity with which these cemeteries, and hundreds of others on the Western Front and around the world, no matter how inaccessible, are maintained.

The CWGC maintains an office at Ypres at 82, Elverdinge Street (this is the road on which St George's Memorial Church is situated). They maintain all the registers for this area here, so should you have sufficient information (name, initials, battalion and regiment and a rough idea of where the casualty was killed) they should be able to direct you to the correct place of commemoration. Other useful items (such as an overprinted Michelin road map with all the cemeteries and memorials overprinted on it) are also available.

I would urge that all visitors take the time to sign the Visitor's Book that is situated in almost all the war cemeteries (normally in the same brass container as the Register). This will give you a chance to express your appreciation, and also help the CWGC maintain their statistics of visitors.

RE Grave Railway Wood. This stands at the approximate final line of the British attack on June 16th. The view is back towards the British line with Ypres in the far distance.

FURTHER READING

The literature of the Great War is massive and the amount of information available to the researcher is encyclopaedic. My intention here is to offer some suggestions of books that are reasonably accessible though, alas, not all of them are in print.

There are a number of personal accounts that provide a real insight into war and its conduct. Amongst these I most strongly recommend *Armageddon Road,* the diary of Billy Congreve VC. This most distinguished officer gives detailed accounts of the early days of the war, and some half of the book concerns the Ypres Salient from the Spring of 1915 onwards. His descriptions of the trenches, of personalities and of events are gripping and opinionated. This gallant officer won the VC — and despite the jaundiced (and often rather ill-informed) opinions of staff officers held by many people, no one could deny that he deserved it.

An observer of a different sort was Private Fraser of the Canadian Expeditionary Force. He provides us with a record of the war from the viewpoint of an articulate member of one of the finest fighting formations of the Great War, the Canadian Corps. It is a remarkably detailed testament, and unusually he has taken the trouble to research and know his facts before expressing opinions. He survived the war, though the diary perhaps lacks the spontaneity of Congreve's, as it was edited in post war years. Nevertheless it is readable, coherent and above all informative.

There's a Devil in the Drum by John Lucy is an eloquent testimony by an Irishman (an NCO) of the war from its early days. It has been out of print for many years, but has been printed once more by the London Stamp Exchange, 1 Old Bond Street, London. It rated extremely good reviews in a period (the 1930s) when books on the Great War were coming out at a rapid rate. It is one of the few that gives a graphic description of life in the army from pre war days (he joined up in 1912 as a private soldier), and he writes vividly of all the early battles, as well as the events around Hooge in 1915.

There are a number of more general guides to the Battlefields available in most of the museums in the Salient. Of a similar nature to this one, but covering much more ground, is my own *Battleground Europe.* This covers a number of Second World War sites (for example Calais and its defence in 1940), but the great bulk of the book is concerned with Ypres and the surrounding area. It is not a guide as such, but details a number of incidents and individuals.

There are a large number of maps, and it is profusely illustrated. It is published by Pen and Sword at £9.95.

John Giles's *Flanders Then and Now* is a new edition of his Ypres Salient. It has plenty of comparison photographs between the War period and modern time, and there are detailed accounts of some actions and some individuals. It is published by After the Battle at £16.95.

Before Endeavours Fade by Rose Coombs MBE also published by After the Battle Publications (about £10 in paperback) is an outstanding guide to the Battlefields of the First World War, and has taken me (and literally thousands of others) to places that we would never otherwise have discovered. The book covers the whole of the British sector of the Western Front, with rather less detailed sections on Verdun and the American sector, further to the south. It is well illustrated.

It might be as well to get yourself a rather more detailed map than the usual Michelin Number 53 that people tend to use in this sector. OS type maps are available (at least the 1:50000 is) at the Tourist Office, housed in the ground floor of the Cloth Hall, Ypres. You can also obtain from there a map of Ypres which makes some attempt to keep up with the nightmareish one way system that has been introduced into the town in recent times.

INDEX

119